FORGOT MEN

Psalm 23

by *Leonard L. Robinson*
LEONARD L. ROBINSON

Printed in Victoria, Canada

Copyright 1987 by Leonard L. Robinson (0-961-9267-0-8). Reprinted 1992.

National Library of Canada Cataloguing in Publication

Robinson, Leonard L., 1919-
    Forgotten men / Leonard L. Robinson.

ISBN 1-55395-078-X

    1. Robinson, Leonard L., 1919-. 2. Prisoners of war—Japan—Biography. 3. Prisoners of war—Philippines—Biography. 4. Prisoners of war—United States—Biography. 5. World War, 1939-1945—Prisoners and prisons, Japanese. 6. World War, 1939-1945—Personal narratives, American. I. Title.

D805.J3R62 2002   940.54'7252'092   C2002-904384-0

TRAFFORD

This book was published *on-demand* in cooperation with Trafford Publishing.
On-demand publishing is a unique process and service of making a book available for retail sale to the public taking advantage of on-demand manufacturing and Internet marketing.
On-demand publishing includes promotions, retail sales, manufacturing, order fulfilment, accounting and collecting royalties on behalf of the author.

Suite 6E, 2333 Government St., Victoria, B.C. V8T 4P4, CANADA
Phone   250-383-6864   Toll-free   1-888-232-4444 (Canada & US)
Fax   250-383-6804   E-mail   sales@trafford.com
Web site   www.trafford.com   TRAFFORD PUBLISHING IS A DIVISION OF TRAFFORD HOLDINGS LTD.
Trafford Catalogue #02-0792   www.trafford.com/robots/02-0792.html

10   9   8   7   6   5   4   3   2   1

Contents

SPECIAL PAGES

COMMANDER OF ALL

Bert O. Sandoval
Written the first week of the war at Fort Stotsenburg

During these many hours of torture,
  While we carefully watch and wait,
Hear the droning enemy raiders,
  We attempt to see our fate.

Never knowing when they are coming,
  Always on the alert,
We beseech our Lord in Heaven
  For forgiveness and for aid.

To alleviate our troubles,
  We look up to Him in prayer
Asking Him for guidance ever,
  And to put our minds at ease.

Nothing ever can be greater
  Than the trust we put in Him;
He will strengthen and will keep you
  But you must have faith within.

Our Commander in His Glory
  Will forsake not one of His.
He will guide us on to victory
  If we do what'er He bids.

Fear not for any troubles,
  For He is all we have,
He's Commander o'er all of us,
  And we're safe from any strife.

INTRODUCTION

Promises! All of us make promises that we hope to keep but sometimes we are kept from fulfilling them by life's problems. I promised many men in prison camp to contact their parents and loved ones if I made it back and they didn't. For over forty years I have searched for these families and talked to others but time is running out so I am writing their story of why they didn't make it home.

This story is based on the lives of soldiers I met in basic training at Fort Bliss in El Paso, Texas, the men I met on Bataan and in the prisoner of war camps. This is their story of why they surrendered, why they gave up after all physical strength was gone, and why they died.

This is the story of a New Testament, a billfold and a list that made it through all the searches by the Japanese during those three and a half years. The Bible was used many times to comfort these men in their final hours. The battered billfold held the few pieces of paper with vital information and the list of men in Battery E of the 200th, who made it through the first attack on Clark Field on December 8, 1941, and dates of death for many.

This is a story of friendships that helped me be one of the survivors of the Japanese prison camps, the hell ships and World War II. But most of all, this is a testimony of the Grace of God toward me in the hours of need. My favorite Scripture was the twenty-third PSALM, and I saw every verse fulfilled in my life. I can only pray that He will sustain and comfort you as you read these words, as He did me as a P.O.W.

I express my appreciation to those who have helped and encouraged me to write this story of my experiences. My children have asked me to write down my memories. I especially wish to express appreciation to my wife for the many hours she spent to help edit the story for publication. I could not have completed the writing without her help. I appreciate the front cover designed by my nephew, Joel Freeland. Thank you to each one for your help and encouragement.

1

CHAPTER I

MY DAY OF INFAMY

PSALM 91:5-7, 11, *"Thou shalt not be afraid for the terror by night: nor for the arrow that flieth by day: Nor for the pestilence that walketh in the darkness: nor for the destruction that wasteth at noonday. A thousand shall fall at thy side, and ten thousand at thy right hand: but it shall not come nigh thee."* . . . *"For He shall give His angels charge over thee, to keep thee in all thy ways."*

The dawn was breaking across the eastern sky and the features of nearby Mount Ararat were taking form in the tropical December morning. Another night on alert was finished near the northeastern edge of Clark Field. The past month was spent in the open air of the starry Philippine sky. It was Monday morning, December 8, 1941 on the eastern side of the International Date Line but December 7th in the United States. This date would change the history of America and most nations, as the world would be plunged into World War II. Yes, there was a war going on in Europe. The German war machine under Hitler had advanced on the neighboring countries and Japan had been at war with China for ten years. America was ferrying planes over to England to help them in the defense of their homeland, but the war still seemed beyond our immediate future.

The Lord gives us many lessons in life. We learn some lessons quickly but the basic principles of life and our fellowship with Him takes a long time. I had read the above verses many times and thought I understood them, but after this day, the entire passage would have a deeper meaning to me. The first part of the verse was fulfilled with the close of guard duty and there was no indication of impending terror.

I finished the last watch of the night (4:00 A.M. until 6:00 A.M.) and guard duty was very boring along the edge of Clark Field. My mind wandered in the darkness of the night, but returned to reality with the breaking of the peaceful dawn at the sight of the parked B-17 bombers. We waved to their guards, as we waited for the 6:00 o'clock hour when guard duty would be over. Each soldier felt some security in the presence of others. The flying fortresses seemed sufficient to protect our shores from any enemy either headed toward or landing on Luzon.

Clark Field and Fort Stotsenburg were sixty miles north of Manila on the Island of Luzon. Our anti-aircraft and some tank units were sent there to increase the military strength of the Philippines. The B-17s were the United States best bombers and had only recently landed on Luzon. Their crews were happy to have the anti-aircraft weapons and our fifty caliber water-cooled machine guns guarding them. We were to give protection on take-offs and landings. The runways of the field were directly in front of us and behind us was the tall cogon grass. The possibility of an enemy slipping upon us was very minute, but we had to be alert for the unknown. We could not imagine war was imminent.

My mind concentrated on the soon end of our tour of duty. First battalion was scheduled to leave in about three weeks and second battalion around January sixth. It would take about three weeks to travel across the beautiful blue Pacific Ocean and arrive back in San Francisco. The men of the National guard were to be discharged the later part of January. A year of military service was required before the outbreak of World War II and three months were all that remained for the fulfillment of my obligations. Then I could return to college for the continuation of my studies.

I was glad for duty in the Philippines because it was a trip I would not have been able to take in civilian life. I had seen many strange and unusual things in the orient during the past three months. All of these experiences would help me when I returned to my studies and to my life's work. Our 200th Coast Artillery (Anti-Aircraft) was originally the New Mexico National Guard. The draftees were mostly from the state of New Mexico but some of us were from other states. This trip was better than participating in the Louisiana maneuvers, or being sent to some other location.

Missions would have a deeper and different meaning to me since I had seen missionaries involved in real life situations with the natives of a foreign country. I had the privilege of spending the first weekend of November in the city of Manila with a missionary family, the Cyril Brooks, who opened their home to American servicemen. There were probably twenty five or thirty servicemen in their home that weekend.

I attended the Sunday morning services at the First Baptist Church of Manila and stayed for a testimony meeting in the afternoon. It was a great blessing and the greatest testimony meeting I have ever had the privilege of attending. Most were school age and lived at the church compound. They told of personal faith in the Lord Jesus Christ and what He meant to them. Most of their parents had disowned and disinherited them because they trusted Christ as personal Savior instead of a church ritual. They walked from their barrios to the city of Manila and lived in the orphanage conducted by the First Baptist Church.

I met one of these "orphans" seven years later when I finished university and entered seminary. I told a Filipino college student that I attended the First Baptist Church of Manila. He told me that he was a student there before the war but fled Manila during the Japanese invasion. He did complete high school and a couple years of college in the Philippines. He won a scholarship to the college in America and planned to return to the Philippines to become a pastor. The need for native pastors in the land of seven thousand islands is very great.

Time seemed to pass faster with my mind active in thought about my stay in the Philippines. Only a few more minutes and I could shout, "Rise and shine." This day I planned to stay in the barracks and attend to some necessary things. I would help Corporal Shields with his duties as Battery Clerk and we would play some chess or ping-pong. I needed to go to the main Post Exchange at Fort Stotsenburg to see Colonel Cook, a family friend. A rest day allowed time to clean up, check on laundry, and write letters. Mail call depended on the arrival of the China Clipper that carried airmail between Manila and San Francisco.

Finally, it was time to forget my daydreams and awaken the men from their sleep on a cloudless morning. Half of our platoon were to go in for early breakfast and cleanup. The rest would stay with the equipment.

The first half moved out for breakfast at a quarter after six. They would return in about an hour and we would dig a little deeper on the foxholes. Our foxholes and all equipment were suppose to be below the surface of the ground. There were several men to a shovel, so our turns on the business end of the shovel were only for a few minutes. We shoveled while it was cool because it was too hot to work in the tropical afternoons. We did not realize that the tropical sun would be the least of our troubles before the end of this day. These same foxholes would triple in depth before sundown but we had a different

4

incentive.

It was past seven thirty and still no sight of our relief. Tomorrow - they will be in a hurry and we will have revenge on them for keeping us waiting! Soon the two trucks came into view around the bend. It did not take long to travel the half mile and we would be on our way to relax. The trucks arrived at the loading area for our trip to the barracks.

What strange stories they had for an excuse! The Japanese had bombed Pearl Harbor! It was unbelievable, they claimed it was a sneak attack and there was a strong possibility our entire Pacific fleet was destroyed. We did not believe their stories and told them so. We thought it was a strange sense of humor to have such an outlandish excuse. We planned to listen to the radio and see if their tales were truth or fiction.

We hurried into the trucks and headed down the edge of the field. We reached the marsh land where we could see bamboo planes parked along the northwestern edge of Clark Field. We wound our way through reeds past the second platoon on the way to the barracks. The last leg of our trip took us past the bamboo planes. We had laughed at them many times and made the remark that if the Japanese should come to the Philippines maybe they would think the bamboo planes were a good target. Our barracks were located between Clark Field and Fort Stotsenburg, but only about a quarter of a mile from the hangers at Clark Field.

The news was true. A sneak attack had taken place at Pearl Harbor and the full damage was unknown but a full assessment was promised later. Great losses were sustained by the Navy at Pearl Harbor and by the Air Force at Hickman Field, as well as the Army at Scofield Barracks. Several ships were sunk and many aircraft were destroyed. We listened with undivided attention to the news which was more important than breakfast. Our schedules were change and we were placed under full alert. There were no arguments or griping about the need to return to our gun positions for continuous duty. The time passed very quickly.

We showered and put on a new uniform because we were not sure when we would be able to return to the barracks. We filled our field bags with the necessities and most important items. I took my full Bible in case we were unable to return to the barracks. I always carried a New Testament in my shirt pocket, but needed the full Bible because many of the verses of

God's protection are found in the Old Testament, especially the PSALMS. I later lost this Scofield Bible with the surrender of Bataan. The only Old Testament I heard in prison camp was read to me by a Jewish man who had his Hebrew Bible.

We never thought the Japanese could pull a sneak attack on the Philippines like they had done in Hawaii. We watched our B-17s and P-40s take off around 7:30 A.M. They would keep watch over the Philippine skies and would spot any Japanese Navy ships off the shores of Luzon. Our B-17s could fly farther than any enemy bombers and they could stop an attack before it started. We thought, there must not be a land base close enough for Japan to launch an attack, or else our B-17s would destroy it. We felt safe for the present time but war would probably eventually come to the Philippines. I remembered the words of a Chinese Christian friend at college, who had told me no country could ever capture China, because it was too large to be conquered and retained. I thought (wishful thinking) that maybe the tide of warfare had turned in China and possibly an attack against Hawaii was a last ditch face-saving attempt to find a solution. I thought our involvement and our active participation would depend on the outcome of the other fronts.

Sergeant Rogers told us it was time to return to our positions. The trip back to our fifty caliber gun position seemed longer than usual. We wanted to listen to the news from Manila but small portable radios were unknown. The only communication was the field telephone with our battery headquarters. Sergeant Rogers gave us our instructions to continue digging on our foxholes until about 11:00 o'clock. He said, "Robinson, Schmid, and Saunders: you are still responsible to go in for the noon meal, so plan to be ready to leave around twelve o'clock." He permitted the two of us on the last shift of guard duty to take off a half hour early to rest.

At eleven-thirty I went to my shelter half-tent and stretched out to relax. My mind analyzed the news reports of the day. How long before we would be involved in the conflict? It would definitely effect my plans because we would not be able to return home until the war ended. Our hopes for a short war would depend upon the purpose of the attack upon Honolulu. I would find out more when I went in for the noon meal and listened to the radio. When the others were dismissed, those in platoon headquarters did not come over to our tent area but stayed around the control box. I relaxed knowing that a believer should be thankful for a peace which passes all understanding. The silence was peaceful and I went to sleep in the middle of the day for the first time as an adult.

The next sound was the roar of the truck as it moved away from the position. I came out of my tent to see why I was not called to go with the other two men. The truck was headed along the north side of Clark Field. I yelled to them but the roar of the motor drowned out the sound of my voice. My chase of the truck ended in what I thought was utter defeat because I had slept through the opportunity of going to the kitchen for a hot meal and now I would have to wait for a cold lunch.

Our planes had landed while I was asleep. The last ones were headed to their parking areas along the edge of the field. Their return gave proof that there were no enemy planes or ships close enough to attack Clark Field and we could feel secure for the present time. The truck with Schmid and Saunders was only a couple hundred yards from the bamboo planes.

Our attention was diverted by the roar of planes in the western skies toward the Zambales mountain range. We thought they were some of our Navy planes which followed the P-40s back to Clark Field. There were two V-shaped formations of twenty-seven planes each. The formations were one behind the other like a flock of ducks headed toward their northern rangeland. The silver color reflected the sunlight to give a beautiful sight but suddenly the bellies of the planes turned from the flittering silver to a dull black. We wondered at the sudden change of color, but our question was answered with emphasis! The first explosions were near the bamboo planes and the explosions were speeding toward us at the speed of the planes flying above us. No, they were definitely not planes of the United States Navy, but bombers of the Imperial Japanese Air Force. We dove for our shallow foxholes and realized the importance of having them deeper, much deeper.

The Japanese heavy bombers were past. The B-17s on either side of us had suffered hits and were burning. It looked like our position should have been hit because of the spacing of the bomb craters but we had been spared. The flying shrapnel had missed all of the men in our platoon. Our greatest concern centered on the two men going for the noon meal and it would be some time before we would know their fate. We had lost a parked truck, but vehicles can be replaced. Flames licked the skies and explosions rocked the area. Many were wounded or killed without a chance to escape in this opening raid. Many airplanes were burning or blown apart, but the greatest loss were those men sent into eternity.

The reprieve to collect our thoughts was short because the bombers had hardly faded into the northeastern sky when dive bombers and pursuit planes arrived to add to the damage started by the heavy Mitsubishi bombers. Some of our P-40 pilots attempted to become air-borne to pursue the Japanese planes but I saw a couple crash on take-off. One hit a bomb crater and the other hit a burning plane, but these men were brave in their effort. The smaller Japanese Zeros flew back and forth across the field. The Japanese pilots had fulfilled their plans; excellent for them but disastrous for us. They ruined almost every plane at Clark Field by bombs or bullets. They fired a number of rounds of ammunition and we returned fire with our rifles and machine guns. Our third platoon was credited with downing a couple of Japanese planes. One Japanese pilot must have spent some time in the United States because he leaned out of his cockpit and thumbed his nose at us. It was estimated between seventy and seventy-five Zeros had followed the fifty-four heavy Mitsubishi bombers.

The middle verses at the beginning of this chapter fell into place. Our destruction did arrive at noontime and many arrows or bullets flew past us along with pieces of shrapnel. Many lives had been taken in the initial attacks on the Philippines. Definitely, and without question, His angels watched over me in the beginning of the conflict.

Fires burned around Clark Field and the surrounding area. The smokey air gave nauseous odors. Our foxholes were deeper, but our first battle of the war was over. We had some close calls and we had escaped physical scars but all of us would have scars in our memory from this first day of combat. Two of our men were still missing and probably casualties.

Two air force enlisted men walked over to our position carrying a rifle and shotgun. They were originally from near New York City and had never been given instructions on the use of guns. We gladly gave them instructions on the use and upkeep of their guns, as the four gun crews took turns cleaning their machine guns and the rest of us ran a patch through our rifles. We watched the sky for unwanted visitors because our telephone system was destroyed. We expected more bombings and did not intend to be caught off-guard.

Colonel Reardon, our Commanding Officer, walked out to our platoon about an hour after the raid was over. He had visited the other two platoons and he wanted to learn our welfare. None of us had sustained injuries or wounds during the attack but we told him about Schmid and Saunders. He sadly told us that a bomb had hit at the left front fender and another had hit near the right rear of the truck.; Both men were instantly killed and the truck was blown apart by the two almost direct hits. The first bombs hit near the bamboo planes and our friends were a short distance from there. They were among the first killed at Clark Field, which was the first place hit in the Philippines. Our battery had a couple wounded but there were many casualties at Clark Field. Almost a hundred were killed and around one hundred fifty wounded on this first day. The destruction was an awful sight.

The sun was sinking low in the western sky and the normal beautiful sunset would be over shadowed by the smoke of burning planes and buildings. We lost most of our three dozen B-17s and over fifty P-40s at Clark Field. Our air power was destroyed and the actual defense of the Philippines faded into obscurity in the fires of those planes. We watched with heavy hearts at the close of this first day of combat.

Our surprises of the day were not finished. Supper was brought out by men of another Battery and they carried orders that the two remaining trucks were to bring half the men to the barracks with all their possessions. We considered ourselves orphans because now we would have to depend upon someone else for transportation. Sergeant Lee was in charge until an officer was appointed. We were left with some questions which would not be answered for a while! One question was never answered. After hearing the reports about Pearl Harbor, why didn't our B-17 bombers leave and bomb the Japanese air force on Formosa?

All Americans alive on that day in December 1941 can probably tell you where they were when the Japanese used the sneak attack while their ambassador was talking peace in Washington. Franklin D. Roosevelt said this was the day that would live in infamy.

I also had unanswerable questions. Why was my life spared when I should have been in the truck destroyed by the direct hits? The Lord had a reason to spare my life, and I would never doubt His watchcare over me. I had been bought with the price of His shed blood and now I must glorify Him in all I say or do. If He could spare my life after the events of this first day, then He could bring me through the entire war so I could serve Him.

We were exhausted at the close of the day but out talks were more serious and our prayers more sincere. We thought of the heartaches and broken dreams of the families of those killed-in-action. The guards walked their posts in a military manner with a different attitude. We realized that it was only by the grace of God that we were alive and not among the casualties.

CHAPTER II

THE BATTLE ENDS ON BATAAN

COLOSSIANS 1: 9-10, *"That ye might walk worthy of the Lord unto all pleasing, being fruitful in every good work, and increasing in the knowledge of God: Strengthened with all might, according to His glorious power unto all patience and long suffering with joyfulness."*

The sun did arise the next morning. The events of December the eighth were reality and not a nightmare. Some of the experiences of basic training were brought into practice: prepare for any hardship, hurry up and wait, do not expect anything to follow a time schedule, and expect the unexpected. We felt secure in our position but the truck drivers delivering our meals wanted to leave as soon as possible.

We had stayed in this vulnerable location for about a week when Lieutenant Hartford was sent to our platoon. He was formerly the First Sergeant of another battery but was one of the enlisted men of the National Guard, who was given a battlefield commission. Sergeant Rogers was transferred the first night and Sergeant Lee became our senior non-com but he later received a battlefield commission. Then Sergeant Williams became the senior sergeant of our platoon. After the division of the 200th, we had only enough men to man the guns plus three men and two non-coms in platoon headquarters.

We soon learned that when a plane took off or landed at Clark Field, it was not long until some unwanted and uninvited guests would disrupt the contours of the landing area. Everyday seemed like a carbon copy of the previous day. We would rise shortly before sunrise after taking our turns on night guard duty. The Japanese used the sunrise or sunset to their advantage. The Japanese would dive so that we would have to look into the sun. This was especially hard because we were without sunglasses.

I was in platoon headquarters and was assigned to the telephone. This gave time to read the Scriptures while I waited for any pertinent information which was needed to be passed on to the others. We were required to be in the immediate area, and be ready to fire our guns instantly. Somebody was always watching the sky for any planes. One of my responsibilities was to identify the planes. Like Ivory soap, 99.44% of the time they were Japanese!

A couple of days after the initial attack I was told to return with the kitchen truck to Battery headquarters to help our Battery Clerk, John Shields, with some records. The Japanese had bombed many buildings at Clark Field and Fort Stotsenburg. My barracks received a direct hit but I was able to salvage some of my personal belongings. I took a hot shower which was my last one until we were liberated three years and nine months later. Shields and I each made a battery roster in case our records were destroyed during the war. We were told later that USAFFE (United States Armed Forces in the Far East) confirmed that the Insurance Applications had gone through to Washington.

The men taken from the 200th on the first night of the battle were made into the 515th Coast Artillery (Anti-Aircraft) and were taken to Manila to protect the capital city of the Philippines. We saw them later on Bataan and they were with us in the various prisoners of war camps.

A couple of trucks showed up at our position from Battery B about a week after the beginning of hostilities. We loaded all of our personal things and equipment into their trucks. Our presence at the edge of the field was unnecessary and we were going to a three-inch gun battery to give them protection from dive bombers. The other two platoons of Battery E were assigned to the other three-inch gun batteries. My chief obligation was the control box which directed the four machine guns. It was designed for a semi-permanent position and now that we were mobile, it was considered excess baggage and we buried it in its foxhole. When we moved from the edge of Clark Field the three or four B-17s Flying Fortresses left Luzon never to return and all that remained were a few P-40s. Air strength was for all practical purposes non-existent.

We arrived at Battery B and set up our position about a hundred and fifty yards from them. We were beside a rice paddy north of Clark Field but in the Japanese line of flight toward Clark Field. The identification of planes was part of the basic training of the control operators so I became a spotter to give the direction and identification of any incoming planes. One time I was thankful to be able to save a couple pilots of the Philippine Air Force from receiving the fire of our four machine guns at close range. Someone yelled to commence firing at the planes but I was able to identify them as an old type American plane (P-26).

12

We witnessed a few crashes, dog-fights, and the downing of planes which we saw hit by anti-aircraft shells. We were near the edge of Clark Field when we saw a B-17 returning to Clark Field with Japanese Zero on its tail. A trail of smoke came out of the B-17. A couple more Zeros entered the picture and began to circle the drifting parachutes. We heard machine gun fire and believed the Zeros were firing at the descending parachutes. The B-17 crashed in the direction of Mount Ararat. We heard this was the plane piloted by Captain Colin Kelly, who rode his exploding plane to the ground. I never heard how many of his crew escaped but we felt sorry for them being shot at under the canopy of their parachutes.

One night we moved to a new position. The next morning, a group of three Japanese planes headed over us on their way to Clark Field. They were flying in a horizontal line when suddenly they changed into a vertical line at about the same time Battery B fired several rounds. One round exploded between the top and middle plane. Immediately, the middle plane began to smoke and we watched it go down. Soon the other two began to smoke and later we heard both had crashed. Naturally, we were very excited that one shell had brought down three planes.

Chilling but expected news was received from headquarters. The Japanese finally made a successful landing on the eastern side of Lingayen Gulf. Our Air Force was so decimated that it was impossible to give the defenders any air protection. Most of the defenders on the eastern shore of Lingayen were members of the Philippines Army, who had only a very short time to become acquainted with the old obsolete rifles issued to them. They made a valiant effort against the experienced well-disciplined invaders but the Japanese were soon moving south along the main highway between Baguio and Manila.

We moved every night or two and we were becoming experts on the use of the shovel. The guns and other equipment of Battery B moved first; then a truck or two were sent back for us. Therefore , we usually were not dug in by the rising of the sun. This gave some very anxious moments, especially when we would hear the drones of airplanes.

One of our problems was with the old ammunition issued to us. The United States had gone through a period of isolation during the 1930s. The prevailing idea was that if we did not manufacture new weapons and ammunition, then the other nations would disarm. America was said to be "big enough" to lead the world in peace--after all wasn't World War I the war to end all wars! The propaganda was that the common people did not want war and American could lead a "peace movement" by not manufacturing munitions. Several large newspapers said that if we would not make any preparations to defend ourselves, the common people of all nations would force their governments to stop making munitions. The result would be a forced world wide peace. The idea was bought by many "good but gullible" people. We know that there will be no world wide peace until the world is ruled by the Prince of Peace, the Lord Jesus Christ in His millennial reign.

The result of this isolation and disarmament almost caused us to lose our freedom permanently because the Axis powers and Russia had the newest munitions and were stockpiling materials needed for warfare. Reluctantly, America began to make some preparations for the update of our armaments. I was among the first men drafted for a year and most of our training at Fort Bliss was with broom sticks simulating the larger guns. We were fortunate to fire 30 caliber machine guns but those on the 37mm and three inch guns were unable to fire any practice rounds before actual combat. We had received our guns shortly before we left the States. Part of the reason, we were in the Philippines was to take the weapons over there and turn them over to their army. We had received the trip because the 200th had the best record on the firing range made with the use of 30 caliber machine guns.

The lack of training on modern equipment was not the worst thing to happen to us. The shells used by our three inch guns were manufactured around the time of World War I and most of them were duds. One out of every four or five rounds would explode in the air. It was very discouraging to watch the three inch guns fire a salvo of a dozen rounds and only two or three burst in the air. Corregidor was prepared for warfare with the type of guns in existence before World War I. The largest guns used against an invasion were all facing the ocean so they could fire on battleships or other man-o-wars attempting to enter Manila bay. They could not be rotated to face an enemy invading from land. When the Japanese attacked Corregidor from Bataan, these largest cannons were worthless. There were a few 90mm anti-aircraft guns on Corregidor but the other obsolete guns and the out dated ammunition cut their effectiveness to about twenty percent. Materials from a fresh arsenal would have helped and given us more potential for protection,

The P-40s were fairly new to the Philippines and they were a much faster plane than the previous planes in the Philippines. The six guns on them caused problems because most pilots had never fired a practice round to text the guns. The P-40s were faster than the Japanese Zeros but experienced American P-40 pilots in China learned to hit and run because the Zeros were superior in maneuverability. The information learned in China was not given to the American pilots in the Philippines and this lack of communication was expensive in battle. The tanks had arrived in the Philippines in the past couple of months. These are some prime examples of being unprepared and having to mobilize at the last minute. We all hope there will never be another world wide war, or even one in which the United States will be involved, but we should not be totally unprepared, as we were in 1941.

Our situation looked bad. We were moved away from the Clark Field area and were told that it would be dynamited. Later, we would feel the tremors and see the flames from the explosions. It was sickening because we knew the gas, ammunition and other war supplies were destroyed. An officer in our battery borrowed a truck and returned to Clark Field. He risked his life to get some ammunition and he divided it between our three platoons. We had already given a report to the regimental supply officer of the amount of ammunition on hand. The officer, who appropriated the extra ammunition, suggested that we keep two accounts of the shells; legal and illegal. Every day we gave an account of the ammunition fired. Sometimes a few minutes after a Japanese raid, the phone would ring and the Lieutenant had to report the amount of ammunition used. He would give an answer about forty percent of the actual amount fired, but even that would bring a rebuke for us to save ammunition.

One day toward the end of the battle for Bataan, a staff officer started to complain about wasting ammunition and admonished us that we should be sure the planes were in range before firing. Our officer replied, "Sir, one of our men held out a match and lit it on the wing of the plane as it flew past. Sir, do you think we let the planes get close enough?" The phone went silent and we had no more static over the hundred rounds reported for that raid.

The Japanese moved south toward Manila and on Christmas day we received an order to move out immediately. The machine gun platoon was moved first for a change but we were dumped temporary at the kitchen of our Battery E. Our kitchen served a breakfast of a spoonful of scrambled eggs with a cup of strong black coffee. We were given two biscuits about the size of a silver dollar; one for dinner and one for supper. Someone asked the cook if he did not have something to put in the biscuit. The answer was quite emphatic, "Why don't you have a jam sandwich? Break the biscuit in half and jam it together." This would be our last meal for a while and Christmas had become a fast day instead of a feast day! It was mid afternoon by the time the trucks returned for us. We had an eerie feeling for the next couple of hours until we were dug into position. We were thankful to the Lord for His watchcare over us.

The Japanese expanded their offensive between Christmas and New Year's because they were trying to reach Manila before the end of the year. We moved our position every night and our only hope was to holdout long enough for the United States to send reinforcements. Most of us realized it would take time, especially after Pearl Harbor, but we hoped that supplies would arrive before the rainy season. The Japanese controlled the sea lanes for over a thousand miles in all directions because the "strongholds" in the Orient had fallen into their hands. Our leaders probably desired to encourage us but some of the rumors which came over the telephone communications were ridiculous. One claimed General McArthur made a statement, "Do not worry because the skies over Manila will be black with American planes and there will be thousands of troops arriving in Manila by New Year's Day." The statement was partly correct, but all of the planes and troops were Japanese instead of American.

The last day of the year we were guarding the bridges at Calumpit over the Pampanga River. Calumpit was located about eight miles southeast of San Franando. It was necessary to keep these bridges open for those coming out of Manila and heading for Bataan. At last, orders were given to cross the bridge before the engineers set their explosives to destroy them. We were the last to cross the Pampanga River before the bridges were destroyed.

All the men of the machine gun platoon were crowded into the back of one truck with one of the machine guns set up in firing position in case of an attack by a dive bomber. The Japanese had been bombing the city of San Franando and the smell of burning flesh added to the tragic sight and turmoil of burning buildings and explosions.

The only road into Bataan began at San Franando. The city and several miles west of town were a sad and pathetic sight. The confusion of the armed forces was bad because of uncertainty and disorganization. Many only knew they were headed for some place on the Bataan peninsula. The road was crowded with all kinds of motor vehicles; trucks, cars, buses, jitneys, calesas, cabs and other vehicles such as bicycles, ox cars and horse drawn wagons. These were piled high with people and personal belongings. I felt sorry for the many Filipino families plodding down the road with all their earthly possessions in a pack on their backs. Many were trying to carry the younger children while the older children tried to keep up with their parents. Their walk was only as fast as the slowest child. Pleading but hopeless eyes carried the message of a desire to still be in the land of the living after this night was history. The sides of the highway were full of discarded articles which had become too heavy to carry. All of us had a common goal -- escape from the oncoming Japanese forces and the indefinite future if captured by them. We were headed into an unknown future with most possessions gone forever.

I was glad for some of our basic training at Fort Bliss and on the desert north of there. The discipline and hardships helped to prepare us for the life we would face in the following days. One night on our tour of New Mexico before going to the Philippines we drove from Deming to Silver City with only black-out lights. The trip was made at a snail's pace but it did help prepare us for the blackout drive on this New Year's eve. The black-out was to protect us from any Japanese night raiders who could have stopped the retreat into Bataan. A few bombs on this only road to Bataan would have halted our withdrawal and we would have been at their mercy sooner.

I had a close call on this New Year's morning. We were very crowded in the back of the truck and were seated around the machine gun. I was sitting uncomfortably on the tail gate when I raised up to change positions when a branch of a tree missed the cab of the truck but it hit me on my helmet. I was flipped out of the truck but I landed on my feet. I reached up and caught the tailgate. I was able to pull myself back into the truck with the help of several men. The trucks were traveling close together and if I had fallen onto the highway, I would have probably been killed or seriously injured by the following

17

heavy truck. I could again know without a shadow of a doubt, "The Lord is my Shepherd."

The individual soldier on the front line was associated with only a small area of combat. I am sure our commanding officers at regimental level were kept informed about the entire operation involving his command. The amount allowed to filter down to the individual serviceman was almost nil. The officers at battery or company level received their orders through the chain of command. Our Lieutenant told us most of the information he received, and since I helped maintain telephone communication, I heard the conversations. Some code was sent over the telephone to be used by certain personal who rated a code book. We tried to pick up the code and were able to figure out some of it. An often used code statement, "Red sails in the sunset." It meant that a Japanese plane (bomber or fighter plane) was taking off from Clark Field and probably headed for Bataan.

I do not know the definite figures of the number of American and Filipino men on Luzon nor have I heard any reliable figures on the Japanese forces. I have read there were approximately the following number of troops on Bataan. There were around 12,500 men and officers from the United States. The Philippine Scouts had around 8,000 outstanding and well trained men and officers. Most of their officers were American but they had some Philippine officers. The Philippine Army had been recently called into service for the emergency and had practically no training in the use of weapons or discipline. Their lines were the first to break in the final days on Bataan. They suffered many casualties during the battle and in prison camps. Their weapons were obsolete, poor in quality and few in quantity. There were probably somewhere between 56,000 to 60,000 of them. Our total number of servicemen, American and Filipinos would be around 80,000. I have read that there were more than 10,000 of this number in the hospitals from wounds and diseases at the time of Bataan's surrender.

The first Japanese forces were made up of battle experienced veterans out of China and recruits from Formosa. They had effective "fifth column" on the Islands, because they seemed to know a great deal about the American and Philippine forces. The large landing forces from Lingayen and Lamon met in Manila on New Years Day in 1942. The Japanese thought with the capture of Manila, it would cause all the Philippine Islands to capitulate, so many Japanese soldiers were sent southward to capture the Islands toward Australia.

The success of the Japanese at Hong Kong, Java, Borneo, Malaya, Sumatra, Singapore were fulfilling their dreams of being the rulers of the East. Bataan soon became their "thorn in the flesh" because it left a weakness in their supply lines. It delayed their plans to invade Australia and forced them to bring back some of the seasoned veterans of other Southeastern Asia battles to take this peninsula of Bataan. It gave the Allies time to set up supply lines and eventually bring the final victory over Japan.

Statistics showed that the Japanese brought into the Philippines three to five divisions with the necessary command and service personnel for the final drive. This would mean between 50,000 to 80,000 fresh fully equipped healthy men plus troops already there. The continuous air superiority of the Japanese was an important factor in the war because they were able to bomb at will. General Homma was considered a failure by the Japanese and he returned to Japan in disgrace because he failed to keep the time table that the military government had planned for a complete victory over the Philippines.

The plan to retreat to Bataan was designed several years previous to the outbreak of the war. Bataan is a peninsula on the west side of Manila Bay. Enough rations and supplies were suppose to have been stored to last for a minimum of six months. This was fiction! It appeared that the people responsible for implementing the plan were woefully negligent in their duties because defense positions were not prepared ahead of time, each group had to dig their positions. The food supply was scarce and clothing preparations for rainy season was likewise non-existent. The doctors and nurses moved into hospitals which were only a clearing cut out of the jungle and without permanent buildings. There was little preparation made for preventive or corrective medical supplies.

Our first gun position on Bataan was in the hills overlooking Subic Bay and Olongapo. We remained a couple days and moved almost every night because there were no prepared permanent positions. The Japanese had air superiority and the concentration of our troops in a small area without concrete bunkers made us easy targets. We were not issued any ammunition or other supplies on Bataan. We soon realized that all the machine gun ammunition was in the boxes of legal

19

and illegal ammunition which lined my foxhole. We had a sufficient supply for our machine guns until the surrender because of the officer who had returned to Clark Field for it.

These circumstances could not be changed so it was necessary that we use what we had to the best of our ability. We can apply these principles to the use of our talents. The Lord does not hold us responsible for talents which we do not have but He expects us to use those we have for His glory. "That ye might walk worthy of the Lord unto all pleasing." I had regular Bible studies with the men of the battery. We knew any help would have to come from the Lord - either to spare us or to give us grace to face our earthy end in the Philippines. My thoughts had by this time become almost fatalistic concerning our situation. There was no way out of our problems through our efforts but we would have to do our best by holding out and trust help would come to the Philippines. My thoughts were similar to Paul's in PHILIPPIANS 1:21, "For to me to live is Christ, and to die is gain." I knew I personally had trusted Christ as my Savior at the age of seven and I belonged to Him. It was not my business to tell Him how He should handle His property. I had to submit to His over-all plan with the realization that if He desired for me to live through these days, He was able; but if He wanted to take me home to Himself, that was His prerogative.

The Japanese offensives let up during the latter part of January. We welcomed this respite because we were exhausted from moving so much the first five or six weeks of the conflict. One morning when we were at the edge of a jungle overlooking Manila bay we were issued three cans of type C rations (World War I vintage) and three small cans of hardtack for next six meals or until they returned for us. We heard the drones of the Japanese airplane motors overhead but we were unconcerned about their target for the first time in six weeks. We enjoyed the short time to rest and think.

Battery B had set up their three-inch guns into their semi-permanent site about three quarters of a mile above Bataan Field, the most used airfield on Bataan. Whenever one of our reconnaissance planes returned, we could expect a flight of Japanese bombers to follow it back to the field. A friend of mine was an airplane mechanic and one day he fixed a plane; it doubled our air force! I think six planes were the most we had at any time on Bataan. Japanese bombers usually came in directly over our position on their way to the field. We would watch them open their bomb bays and follow the flight of bombs from their release until shortly before they exploded on the field. The three inch guns would fire at them and if in range we would fire at them.

Our guns were located at some interesting sites. Most of the time they were at the edge of a rice paddy but sometimes it was near a growth of trees or a bamboo thicket or a banana plantation. We never knew what to expect because we were usually dug in by dawn before we could survey and analyze the location.

My first foxhole on the plantation was interesting. It was about dawn when I noticed that a branch remained only a few inches from my face and it would remain a couple of inches away from my eyes. I realized that something was wrong and I had better take a closer look at the unusual branch. Instead of a branch, it was a long green snake with the lower part of its body wrapped around the trunk of the tree but its head was watching me from close range. I stepped away from the foxhole for a few minutes as I considered who had first priority. Later I killed a couple of pythons about twelve feet long in this same general area. I did not want one or both to drop upon me from a tree limb some dark night. One of the longest snakes ever captured was in this part of Bataan.

We were happy with our position on the banana plantation. Four of us were originally put on an outpost near a spring. The first day, I made friends with the owner. This spring was for their drinking water and it was carried about a hundred yards to the house. The Filipino invited me into his home to share a meal with his family. His house was built on stilts about seven feet above the ground so it would not be flooded during rainy season when the water would stand a couple feet deep. The house consisted of two fairly large rooms (sixteen feet square) and was constructed of wooden beams covered with bamboo. The floors were strips of bamboo about an inch and half or two inches wide with an open space of an inch between the strips where scraps of food dropped through the cracks to their chickens. The roof was covered with nipa palm leaves and held in place by pieces of bamboo. The sides of the house were made out of closely woven bamboo swallie.

The inside of the house was interesting. The kitchen, dining room and supplies were in the west room. The east room was used for the living and sleeping areas. The north wall of the living area had a cabinet with the family pictures and keepsakes

21

so that they were farthest from the general direction of the storms. A piece of swallie was laid on the floor and a mosquito net was set up to protect the family from flying insects. Bataan is one of the worst places for the infectious female anopheles mosquito, the carrier of malaria. This type of a house was excellent for the jungles because it gave protection from the floods during the rainy season and was good for any breezes blowing during the dry season.

I talked to my friend about Christ and found he had listened to some of the radio broadcasts from Manila. I hope he and his family made it through the war years. If they survived the Japanese offense against Corregidor then they probably were able to continue to live on their plantation.

One day we were watching a P-40, when a Zero came up behind him. The P-40 headed toward our machine gun position on a north to south course and a little to our west. Our officer gave the command to commence firing at the Zero. The Japanese Zero broke away and headed back north. The pilots at Bataan Field were housed only about a quarter of a mile from our position in the banana plantation. The P-40 pilot came over to thank us for firing at the Zero as he had deliberately led it over our position. His only question was why didn't we fire more rounds. Near the end of the battle on Bataan a number of Japanese Mitsubishi bombers were flying at a height greater than the range of our three-inch guns. Corregidor had some 90mm anti-aircraft guns and we watched a burst hit a bomber in the wing. The wing flew off and the plane plunged like a rock until it exploded in Manila Bay. The victory of one plane going down was enough to give us some encouragement.

One of the greatest concerns on Bataan was food. We were put on half rations when we retreated to the Bataan peninsula. We would eat a meal before sunup and another meal after sundown. This kept the Japanese from bombing us at mealtime. Rations kept declining until we were down to approximately one fourth rations before the surrender. Mules and horses of the 26th Cavalry of the Philippine Scouts were used for food to provide some meat and General Wainwright also gave up his pet horse. There was no refrigeration so we would have to eat the meat as soon as possible after it was delivered. The mule's meat tasted better than horse because it was sweeter. We were glad for some fresh meat, even if, it was in limited supply. There were a few edible animals which included wild boar, wild chicken, monkeys, iguana lizards and other small animals. One of my duties as a scout was to search for food in my spare time.

Monkeys were a logical choice to add to the menu. They were easy to shoot out of the trees but the other monkeys would run through the top branches of the near-by trees chatting and screaming at the top of their lungs. They seemed to rebuke and scold the person who had shot the fallen monkey. The man who skinned the monkey lost his taste for the meat, because the skinned animal reminded them too much of a human infant. The plantation owner showed me the various plants and fruits which were suitable for eating. These included bananas, mangoes, bread fruit, papayas, coconuts, pineapples, star apples, cashew nuts and several others. The blossoms of the banana plants were cut up for a salad. It tasted better with vinegar to sprinkle on it. The bread fruit made us sick at first but later we found out the little white seeds could be boiled and they reminded us of white potatoes. The cashew nut grows underneath a fruit, but my friend said it was poisonous and cashews needed to be roasted before eaten. The acidity of the fruit was very high. Little red peppers about the length of a joint of a person's finger tasted like liquid fire. One pepper would season the entire ration of food for me but some men with a Spanish culture would eat a half dozen at once.

I enjoyed the scouting duties while searching for extra food. The banana plantation owner would sell me bananas for a half cent apiece and I would let the men at our position have them for the same amount. The owner would pick the bananas while they were still green and bury them in pre-dug holes on his plantation. He carefully wrapped them in banana leaves and in a couple of days they were ready for sale. He allowed me to go with him and showed me how to tell when the bananas were ripe enough to eat. The first tree I learned to climb was a papaya tree, which is similar to a palm tree. The tree grows some twenty to twenty five feet above the ground with the fruit in a cluster just below the limbs and leaves. There were usually about a dozen pieces of fruit in the cluster but only about two or three were ripe at the same time. Needless to say, any extra food was a wonderful addition because of the scant rations.

Part of my duties as a scout made it possible to visit several other platoons for Bible Studies. Our chaplain never made it up to our area. I was glad for my Scofield Bible to help in studies and counselling. I was happy for the opportunity and my Lieutenant was willing for me to be gone for these services.

It was necessary to travel in pairs because a single person could be surprised by a Japanese snipper. Bill Moore usually travelled with me. I would take the lead and he would be six to ten feet behind me. We had a few eerie moments along the jungle trails. We travelled in silence but when we both would take our eyes off of the trail for a moment we would hear, "Hello Joe."

An Igorrote Indian dressed in a minimum of clothes, but with bolo (knife), bow and arrows, would walk along the trail with us carrying on a friendly talk using both oral and sign language. Suddenly he would disappear when our attention was distracted for a moment. We could hear no sounds nor see any foot prints because the so-called primitive man was swallowed up in his environment. We were certainly glad for their friendship because we were at their mercy. We could never figure out how they could move so silently in those jungle growths. The Japanese learned to keep out of the jungles because many of their heads were found separated from the body. Psychological warfare puts a lot of pressure on a person especially a bolo in the hands of an unseen Igorrote.

We stayed in the semi-permanent position, except for about a week or ten days, when we were taken up to protect the Filipino Scouts Field Artillery's 155mm guns. These were nicknamed the Long Tom and were approximately six inches in diameter. The Japanese were pouring thousands of fresh troops into the peninsula in order to take Bataan before the start of the rainy season. The Long Toms were helpless against the diving Japanese planes but our machine guns were effective against them. We were kept on a constant alert because while we were watching one group of Japanese planes, another group would slip in on us using the sun for a background.

We talked around our command post while watching the beautiful tropical sky. The stars seemed close enough to touch and I especially heard the sounds of gun fire. All at once the silence was broken as the long projectile of the Long Tom sailed over our heads. The concussion was great enough to raise an army blanket about six feet off of the ground.

A sleepy sergeant yelled, "They are shelling us." He and several others jumped into a foxhole. We had a man who was an excellent cartoonist and we laughed at his cartoon of men diving into a foxhole headfirst under a floating blanket with a projectile travelling overhead. Nunez drew several other excellent cartoons of the war. Later, we heard the Long Toms landed their shells in a school yard where a regiment of Japanese soldiers had bedded down for the night.

The Japanese used an observation plane, which we nicknamed "Maytag Charlie" to keep us awake day and night. These lone planes would arrive about sunset and fly back and forth around Bataan. The length of time was not consistent but sometimes a couple of hours. He finished his first flight by dropping a couple of bombs and then "Charlie" would head for Clark Field. Another "Charlie" plane would arrive and follow the same pattern. We joked about them and said we expected a Japanese photographer to meet our ship at San Francisco, when the war was over and ask us if we wanted to buy our picture which he had taken on Bataan. The odds of being hit by one of these bombs was exceedingly small but the psychological effect fulfilled their purposes. Although one of the bombs did hit a hospital ward. We had our "bed check Charlie" for the three and half months on Bataan.

William Jennings Bryan said that he had yet to meet a man who was not superior to him in somethings. I found this to be true and I learned something from every one I met during the three and a half years as a prisoner of war. I had many interesting acquaintance in my own battery, other servicemen from the 200th, others in prisoner of war camps, civilians and servicemen in El Paso, some Filipino civilians and missionaries in the Philippines. Many people have played an important part in my life. I can not tell about each one, but I would like to mention certain ones. Bert Sandoval, (I believe his father was a Presbyterian Missionary in New Mexico) wrote a wonderful poem on the first day of the war. He entitled it, "Commander of All". One statement, "Nothing ever can be greater than the trust we put in Him;", was the summation of our time overseas.

I recall with pleasure the time spent with some of the Navajos of my battery and regiment. I became personally acquainted with some of the minority people and I am now better able to understand some of their problems. I met men from all of the states in prison camp and I appreciated the part they played in my life. There are no accidents in the life of a believer and I believe each one of these men crossed my life for a purpose.

One evening before the out break of hostilities, a friend came by the barracks and asked if I would like to go to the quarters of the 26th Cavalry of the Philippine Scouts. He had a friend there who had gone through the flagellants, but had come to know Christ as his personal Savior within the past year. The Filipino Scout stripped to the waist and showed us the scars on his arms and body. Scars caused by whips which had bits of metal or pieces of broken glass on the leather straps. The flagellant would whip himself and others would scourge him until he was bloody from head to toes. Each time the whip with pieces of metal or broken glass touched his body, the flesh would be cut. He had volunteered for several years in a row to go through the punishment of a flagellant because he wanted to find a way to have his sins forgiven. His religion told him salvation would have to be by his works and this would help him. The flagellants would be raised on the cross in the hot tropical sun for a short time before being taken down. He would crawl from the outside of the building to a statue of Christ on the inside of the church. While crawling on his knees, he would confess his sins and ask for forgiveness of all his past sins. He lived in a barrio near a river that flowed into Manila Bay where the high tide would cause the river to flow backward. He entered the river at high tide so the salt water would keep infection out of the many wounds on his arms, legs and body. This was supposed to give him forgiveness for his past sins. Because he had returned to his sinful life by the next year, he needed to repeat the procedure. One day he heard the message that Christ died for all sins; past, present and future. He understood for the first time that salvation is by faith and not by works. He realized only the grace of God gives eternal life. All the years as a flagellant were to no avail because finding forgiveness before God is by accepting God's gift. Now, his hope was in the finished work of the LORD JESUS CHRIST.

Friends helped in our daily existence but Japanese snippers influenced our daily life. We ate in a small clearing with breakfast before sunup and supper after sundown. After the meals, we would walk past barrels of hot water and dip our mess kits in them to clean them. One night a cook noticed something strange about two mess kits and realized they were Japanese utensils. He yelled a warning but by that time the Japanese soldiers had faded into the night cover of the jungle. Short rations were bad enough but to have to share them with an enemy was adding insult to injury.

One day a report came that some Japanese snippers were spotted in our area and several of us were sent out to see if we could locate them. I was working my way through the trees when I lost all interest in the Japanese because I felt a sharp pain in a number of places. There is an ant, which we call either a cannibal or telegraph ant, that crawls on your body and then all the ants bite at the same time. It is more of a bite than a sting because they actually took a piece of flesh. When the ants started biting me, I stripped off my uniform so I could pick off the ants and kill them. I wanted to cry because of the pain but shook my clothes and searched for any ant survivors. We did not locate any snippers and I was glad none spotted me when my attention was centered elsewhere.

We were expected to walk our guard duty about every other night in a military manner. We knew it was safer to watch for any movement from a stationary location. An enemy could easily destroy a walking guard. One night at Battery B, a shot was fired and then, "Halt, who goes there?" broke the silence of the night.

A strange silence followed. A dead fox was found the next morning and everyone learned to not try to slip upon a guard near the front lines. You may not have the privilege for a second chance because they shot first and then asked questions.

A sergeant thought it was fun to catch someone resting or not paying attention on guard duty. He tried it one night on another man and me. We did not intend to walk our posts but planned to sit in the middle and watch for any movements. The sergeant started to slip up through the banana trees to try to catch us being careless. We watched him approach our position and both threw a shell into the chamber of our rifles. He yelled his identity and asked us not to shoot. We told him to return to his command post and stay there. When we came off of guard duty, he wanted to know if we would have shot him.

We merely told him, "Sarge, remember the fox and don't try it again." The advice was sufficient and he never tried to slip up on anyone again.

One day while I was at headquarters of Battery E, I learned to appreciate a gun platoon instead of headquarters. The psychological effect of unseen planes did not bother most of the men but a few had a hard time with hearing planes but not being able to see them. I saw one foxhole about fifteen feet deep and the two men practically lived there twenty four hours a day.

27

We were in the open on the gun position because we needed a clearing to fire the guns. We could watch the enemy planes in our area and could take cover when one headed in our direction. The Japanese attacked our position a number of times but the danger from any one plane was only a few seconds. We would watch the plane come in on us and we had only a few seconds to sweat out his bombs or machine gun fire. Then it would be safe until another pilot changed the tranquility of the minute.

One day I hitched a ride with a quarter master truck to Mariveles. Jesse L. Miller, who had been in the photography section in the Air Force was there. We had enjoyed good fellowship before the war and I wanted to see how he was surviving the hostilities. My life seemed destined to be acquainted with this man of God. I would meet Jesse again in Cabanatuan and after we returned to the States. He is one of the many ex-prisoners of war who went into the ministry. He and his wife organized the Christian Overseas Servicemen Centers that has helped many servicemen since World War II. We shared information about our areas and it was plain to see that food and supplies were in short quantities throughout the entire peninsula. It would be impossible to live off of the land for the five months until the end of the rainy season. I hitchhiked back, wiser but less hopeful for our condition.

The situation was more serious after General McArthur escaped in a secret P.T. boat for Australia. His departure carried the dreams that supplies or reinforcements would come before the rainy season. It meant as far as the United States were concerned, we were expendable. Receiving supplies by submarines was in the category of - "let me dream on." The essence of one rumor was correct, "No Uncle Sam, not even an aunt, or any cousins and no one gives a hoot." Spiritually, we could remember, "I am the door by me, if any man enter in, he shall be saved, and shall go in and out and find pasture."

Morale still remained good in spite of the circumstances. We figured we would hold out as long as possible and then prepare for a final fight on the tip of Bataan. Slowly, it entered our minds that Bataan would probably become another Alamo.

We were ill-prepared to fight our second enemy, malaria. Bataan is known to be an extremely infested area for malaria and we did not have any quinine. Mosquito nets were left behind at Clark Field and we realized most would probably be the victims of a malaria-carrying mosquito in the not too distant future. The hospital had many malaria patients but it would get worse with the arrival of rainy season. The short rations were causing us to lose strength so we could only hope to remain well enough for the final battle. The days of our struggle were fast coming to an end and the Philippine Islands would soon be under the control of the Imperial Japanese Empire.

I had experienced several bombs and bullets hitting close to me. Once the Lieutenant and I were in the same foxhole during an attack by a dive bomber. The bomber looked like he was trying to occupy the same foxhole with us. The foxhole was not that large but we were trying to make room when the pilot pulled up at tree top level. I could hear the machine gun bullets hitting fairly close and when the raid was over a couple of bullets were buried in the dirt above my head. I dug them out and stuck them in my bag to bring home for a souvenir but these were among the many things I lost with the surrender of Bataan.

The morning of April eighth started like any previous morning. We knew the Japanese were making a push and there were weak places along our front lines. The constant shellings and bombings were taking their toll in human life and endurance. We were expecting a break in the lines at any moment, so we prepared sand bags to be placed under the tripods of our machine guns. This would elevate them above ground level so that we could use them against ground troops.

The eighth was the last full day of the battle for Bataan. The previous attacks had been in the afternoon from over Bataan mountain, but the first attack on the eighth came from the east with the pilots coming in on the morning sun. We faced nine different dive bombing attacks against our position before the day was over. My foxhole was about seven feet in diameter and was lined with boxes of ammunition. A member of one of the gun crews was near my foxhole when we spotted several Japanese planes go into the sun and start their dive. We both dived into the foxhole and from the concussion I knew a bomb had hit very close. I received a damaged ear drum and the flesh over my heart was hot . I found a piece of shrapnel resting against my rib cage. I carried my New Testament in my left shirt pocket and I have always figured it saved me from a serious injury.

I raised up to see where the bomb had hit and it had landed about three feet from the foxhole with the crater up to the edge of the foxhole. My bed was about fifteen feet away and the shrapnel tore large holes in my blanket, shelter half, and my bed was torn to pieces. I do not think the other man ever knew how close that bomb came to blowing us to eternity.

Front-line soldiers of the Philippine Army were coming through our area by noon. These soldiers were headed for Mariveles and they apologized to us as they hurried to the rear lines. We expected the Japanese troops to arrive at any moment for our last battle.

The last attack by the planes came shortly before sundown. All communications were broken by the middle of the afternoon and the officers of the two batteries had a short conference to decide what they should do. The Lieutenant came to me and said "I am not sending you on this mission but we would appreciate it if you would go to headquarters (regimental) and learn our orders"

I accepted the responsibility but I knew it would probably be close to midnight before I could return because of the narrow jungle trail. I told him how I would whistle, so as to identify myself upon the return.

I walked to my foxhole and did a foolish thing that probably saved my life. I was reared in Colorado and my father had cautioned me that on a long walk to never put on a new pair of shoes. I put on the new shoes, a clean uniform and took the items that I would need for our last stand in case I could not get back to my outfit.

One of the three other men who were to go with me was from my battery and walked directly behind me. The other two were communication men from Battery B who we hoped might be able to repair our communications.

We arrived at regimental headquarters a little before 9:00 P.M. to find trucks pulling out. They were headed for our last stand. Our orders were that the 200th would be on the front lines at Cabcaben. A runner had been sent but I was told to return by the jungle trail in case the runner failed to make it to our position. The other three men went with the headquarters trucks. If the runner was unable to get through, then I would have to lead about a hundred men through the jungle to Cabcaben.

When I whistled my identification, there was no answer. I walked up to the first gun position and found all the men were gone. The runner had arrived and the battery had gone down the road past Bataan Field. They were fortunate to make it to

regain health and strength. We knew a little about the Japanese and wondered about the prospects for the future. As a believer, I knew I would have to place myself in His hands. The Scriptures state, "Casting all your care upon Him, for He careth for you." I knew that there was usually a survivor from every event, and by the grace of God and with His help, I would be a survivor from the Japanese prisoner of war camp.

We had little time to contemplate our ideas, as a dozen tanks surrounded our group of men. They lowered their cannons at us and one tank went behind us to cut off any possible route of escape. Several of the Japanese opened the tank turrets and looked at us. An English speaking Japanese told us to throw our rifles, all ammunition and cartridge belts into a pile in the center of the opening. A couple of men asked a question but we were instructed that any questions would bring a shot from a tank. I parted company with Springfield rifle #57047 and bayonet #208444 which gave me a very depressed feeling. I was surprised that no rifle accidentally fired because all were loaded and I am sure all were not on safety. The tanks could have used an accidental discharge for a reason to annihilate all the men gathered in the opening.

The Japanese were unhappy with us, and we were definitely ill at ease with them. The English speaking Japanese told us to walk down the road to the airfield at Cabcaben, and we would receive further instruction there. I started down the road with only the clothes on my body, a steel helmet, the New Testament and a field bag with a few articles. My new shoes were hurting my feet, but fortunately I had not taken them off.

Japanese guards were along the edges of the field, and the Japanese had brought in some heavy artillery guns on the north side. They began to fire over our heads at Corregidor. The fire was returned with the projectiles landing short of the Japanese guns and hitting on the Cabcaben Field. One shell landed close enough to raise a welt on my arm, and I made a break for the main highway. I figured that after becoming a prisoner, I did not want to be cut down by a shell from Corregidor. I went past several Japanese at the edge of the field and they made no effort to stop me. I am sure that if I had gone toward the jungle, I would have been shot. This was my beginning of the infamous death march of Bataan.

The road was full of hills and curves because most of Bataan was hilly jungle country. Many Japanese infantry groups were headed south along the highway trying to get ready for their coming assault against Corregidor. Some of the artillery groups were pushing their weapons. The prisoners dreaded meeting the tanks, because the drivers would have enjoyed running over prisoners. Some Japanese soldiers did order some prisoners to get in front of their tanks, and then they ran over them.

Each Japanese group treated the recent captives differently. Some were without any reaction but others called us names, which we would not understand but the actions were not complimentary. I was searched many times and almost all of my personal items were taken in the various searches. A soldier would have us lay out all of our things before him, and he would take whatever he wanted. Each search was an individual ordeal which usually ended up by being slapped or beaten. Sometimes they were very angry if they could not find a certain item. They were especially anxious to find jewelry.

I ended the march with the clothes I was wearing; a steel helmet, the field bag with a notebook, a canteen cup, my battered billfold with a little American money in its hidden pocket, and a cut off tablespoon. I was glad for my worn and tattered billfold because new billfolds were taken immediately. Some were disgusted with me because they could not find any money in the billfold, but probably figured someone else had taken it. I used the notebook for a diary from the time we left for over seas but I had destroyed all except the roster of Battery E. The cut off spoon was given to me by someone who had an extra spoon.

I had an exceptionally close call during one of the first searches, but did not realize how dangerous it was to cause a Japanese man to "lose face". He had me lay out my possessions and there was nothing of interest to him. He took my New Testament from my shirt pocket. He looked at it, spoke some angry words, and threw the New Testament to the ground. I reached down, picked up the New Testament, dusted it off and looked him straight into the eyes. We stared at each other for a few moments before he walked away toward the south, and I continued down the road out of Bataan with trembling knees. I realized the seriousness of my actions and later saw others killed for a lesser offense so I know it was only the grace of God I was not killed on the spot.

Travel was slow and crowded. I was forced to help push some field artillery weapons to the top of the next hill, and then retrace my steps. Some truck and tank drivers would turn their vehicles toward me, and I would have to get off the road. I knew from sign language that I would be a victim of a bayonet if I tried to go very far off the road. I was hit with sticks, bamboo poles and rocks. Twice on this first day of the march I was hit with a rifle butt as a truck passed me. My steel helmet took the main force of the blow, but once I was knocked to the ground.

A few miles north of the junction to Bataan Field, a Japanese non-com called twenty two of us over to the side of the road. He took us over to the edge of a bluff and had us line up. He had a Japanese soldier face each one of us.

The bluff dropped straight down for about fifteen feet, and then sloped away from us. The total drop was fifty to sixty feet, and there was dense jungle at the bottom of the bluff. I had held a Bible class in the vicinity and knew the area. I decided that when the order to fire was given, if my man did not shoot first, I would fall over the bluff and hit it rolling. If I survived the fall, I would make a dash for the jungle. It was almost night and would give me good cover. I could easily arrive at the banana plantation by morning and the next day continue into the deep jungle. The soldiers loaded their rifles, threw a shell into the chamber, and their fingers came upon the trigger. A Japanese officer stepped out of a house and yelled at the non-com. I do not know what was said but the soldiers took their rifles off their shoulders. He motioned for us to beat it down the road, and we did not ask him to repeat his order.

We picked up extra guards during the night time but the oncoming troops could not see us in the darkness, so the abuse and searches subsided. The guards seemed to change every couple hours. We marched into the city of Limay around 4:00 o'clock on the morning of the tenth and were herded into a corral. We would be able to sleep until 6:00 o'clock when we would be awakened to continue the march. A water faucet was near the entrance of the corral, and I was able to receive my first cup of water in twenty-four hours.

I was delighted to be reunited with two friends, Bill Moore and Cecil Uzzel. (Both were assigned to our Battery at Fort Bliss in July, 1941.) Cecil remained in service until he could retire and he helped organize several Baptist churches in Germany among servicemen. It was the Lord's will that Cecil and I would be together all through the war and in the prison camps. Cecil, Bill and I tried to help each other, and each of us were able to survive as long as we did because of help and encouragement of the others. Cecil especially helped me through the illnesses which I had at Niigata, Japan. Bill Moore was also a believer and he perished when his P.O.W. ship was sunk. My feet were hurting after walking two nights and a day, so I took off my shoes. I used them for a pillow, as we were crowded together and there was no room to move or even to change position.

We were awakened at sunrise and told to prepare to move out. We wanted to be near the front because it was an advantage to be near the head of the column of marchers. It was easier for oncoming Japanese to hit the front row with clubs but the front men set the pace. If you could not keep up with the leaders you could gradually drop back toward the end of the column. Most of the men had moved out of the compound before my shoes were found. I was certainly happy to find my shoes because I was afraid that someone else was wearing them. I hurried to get them on my feet, but we were among the last ones to arrive at the gate.

The guard closed the gate on the last thirteen of us and we wondered if they would make an example out of us. I was glad Cecil and Bill stayed with me, but I wondered if I would cause them to receive a beating. We could imagine all sorts of bad things that would happen to us.

The entire place had a bad odor from the accidents of nature by the sick men. The straddle trench latrine was crawling with maggots. This would become a common condition we would face all the time in the prison camps in the Philippines. Each place used to provide overnight sleeping compounds for the POWs marching out of Bataan grew steadily worse each night.

They took us out of the corral at mid-morning and placed us with a group of fifteen officers: three full Colonels and the others were Captains or higher. We rode the rest of the way out of Bataan to San Fernando. The Lord used my mistake of putting on a brand new pair of shoes to possibly save our lives. Truly, "The Lord is my Shepherd."

The three of us did have an easier time than those men who walked the entire route, but we still suffered and saw many atrocities. The guards had already questioned the officers. We were placed in the back of a truck and taken to Pilar. A Japanese officer questioned us about our tasks in our military unit. We had been told that all we had to give was our name, rank and serial number which was all we gave to him.

We were taken to an open field with other prisoners of war. A couple of guards kept a close watch on the twenty-eight of us while we received our first sun treatment. We were forced to get on our knees and told to take off any caps, hats or helmets. We had to maintain an upright and stiff position with the fingers extended downward. The heat soon affected us and we started to slump. The guards had clubs and hit us on the head if we did not remain at a rigid stiff attention. Some prisoners did keel over because of the heat, and most of us tried to relax when a guard was not in the immediate area. Over an hour later, our guards took the twenty-eight of us away. We were loaded into a truck and taken to the city of Balanga.

We were placed in the city jail at Balanga. The sidewalk was on all four sides, so the people could see us, and it was here that we saw the courage of the Filipino people. They tried to give us some food but the Japanese guards kept them from it. We were allowed to have a little water and after dark the Filipinos threw us some rice balls and other food which we devoured.

Bataan is a peninsula about seventeen miles wide by about forty miles long. The main road went down the east side, across the south side, and about halfway up the west side. The southern and western sides are covered with thick jungle and deep ravines which made the western side almost inaccessible. The only other road was the cobblestone road which runs between the two main mountains of Bataan. Mount Natib is on the north and Mount Samat is on the south sides of this road. The agricultural section of Bataan is in the northeastern part of the peninsula.

Balanga was near the junction of the two roads on Bataan. The prisoners captured on the western front were brought across on the cobblestone road to Balanga. All prisoners spent one night in Balanga. The bad treatment received up to Balanga seemed to be a spontaneous action committed by the individual soldiers, but from Balanga on to O'Donnell, the brutalities were encouraged by some higher ranking officers.

Some of the major battles of Bataan were fought around Balanga. The scars of the battle were revealed by the smoldering jungle, blackened stumps, stripped trees and destroyed foliage. The sides of the road were covered with discarded military equipment, destroyed vehicles, discarded clothing and signs of atrocities. The captives struggled slowly along the road because of illness and weakness. There were many men bayonetted because they were too weak to continue to march.

Some Filipinos smuggled food to us in the morning at the risk of their lives. The officers were taken one at a time to a headquarters and then the enlisted men were questioned. I was among the last to be interrogated by the Japanese officer. I was amazed at the amount of information he knew about the American forces. He was acquainted with most of the army organization, but did not know the size of the units. He told me I was a draftee because of my serial number and guessed that I was in the 200th Anti-aircraft. He did not try to force any information from me because the Japanese officer did not expect enlisted men to have vital information because Japanese culture only respected officers. We were taken back to the jail; then, we were taken out to an open field around noon for another sun treatment. Later, we were loaded onto the trucks and taken up the road to Orani.

The night of the eleventh was spent in the jail at Orani. The Filipinos showed their kindness by smuggling food to us in spite of the Japanese guards. I was surprised at the attitude of the Filipinos who had suffered so much, but who were willing to share their limited food with us. They certainly proved their courage and loyalty. The guards were able to keep the later marchers from receiving any food from the Filipinos.

The first order of business for the next day was another interrogation session by a Japanese officer. The officers were questioned first and then the enlisted men were questioned for a short time. We finally departed from the jail around noon for another sun treatment. We still had several shake downs, but I had already lost most of my things, so had no reason to worry. Officers were searched especially for college rings and a West Point ring was the key prize for a Japanese officer to confiscate.

The new shoes had spared me from much of the death march, but everything I have read or heard about the march I either saw personally or heard about it from eye witnesses. I have seen men break ranks to get water from a mud puddle. I have watched the Japanese soldiers toss water on the ground rather than allow a POW to have a sip of the precious liquid between his parched lips. This happened to me when my thirst was agonizing and they would laugh because of the disappointment expressed on my face. Many men made the march of a week to ten days without food or water. Many could not continue because of the diseases contracted before the fall of Bataan, or from the contaminated water drank along the march. Men were helped or carried by others because they could not move on their own legs any longer. A friend of mine was forced to cover up men too ill to continue the march. He and the others who were with him refused, and were told to cover them up or be covered up with them.

The twenty-eight os us boarded the truck and were taken to San Fernando. It had been three months since we went thru the city on our way into Bataan but the scars and damages were still evident. We were taken to a large arena that was used for cockfighting. We were among the first to arrive, but soon others began to come into the building and we were told to stay as a group by a couple officers out of the 200th. Some of the Japanese guards seemed friendly and several wanted to trade with us. Most of us had only necessities, but one of the officers out of the 200th traded something to a guard for a Japanese coin.

The "death march" officially ended in San Fernando. We were captured on the front and it was about sixty-five miles from Cabcaben to San Fernando. Some of the men were captured where the distance of the march was about one hundred miles. It has been estimated that approximately 10,00 American and Filipino troops died on the march. It was reported that close to a thousand were American. This does not include the number of civilians killed by accident or design. Starvation, weakness, malaria, diarrhea, dysentery and other diseases took their toll.

San Fernando was a rail center, and the next morning one hundred men were put into each narrow gauge boxcar that was about seven feet wide, thirty feet long and approximately seven feet high. We were packed so tightly that everyone had to stand. The doors of the boxcars were closed and we began our journey north from San Fernando. The heat, stench of vomit and those with diarrhea was unbearable. Men fainted but remained in an upright position because there was no place to fall. Several men died on the five or six hour trip to Capas. It was mid-afternoon when we arrived in Capas and we began the five mile walk to Camp O'Donnell.

Major Reardon was one of the fifteen officers on the trip out of Bataan. Once a Colonel received some eggs which he divided with the officers and Major Reardon divided his with the three of us. The Major, Cecil, Bill and I marched together from Capas to O'Donnell. The Filipinos met the train, and some of them followed us out of town throwing food to us. If any of the four of us caught some food, we divided it with the other three. We were glad for some pieces of sugar cane because it gave us moisture for our lips and throat. Some pieces of sugar cane had also helped me on the march out of Bataan.

Officers like Major Reardon helped to increase the number of survivors from prison camps. Sorry to say, we had some of the other kind. It was a shame that many men and officers were only concerned about themselves and in some cases caused the death of others while trying to secure help for themselves.

Camp O'Donnell came into view and the first impressions were far too accurate. We would learn that this was no place for man or beast. I was among the first prisoners to arrive at O'Donnell on April thirteenth. The Lord had done exceeding abundantly above all that I asked or thought in surviving the march.

It was a good thing that we were unable to look into the future. The recently completed death march would go down in history as an example of extreme brutality and inhuman treatment but the following six weeks in O'Donnell would be forgotten by the majority of historians. It would only be remembered by the participants. Even our own government in order to appease the Japanese after the surrender denied the vicious treatment received in the Philippines. A couple of years ago the truth was finally revealed by the Chinese historians. This forced our government and the media to tell some of the true story.

CHAPTER IV

LIFE IN O'DONNELL

I PETER 3:8, 12a, *"Finally, be ye all of one mind, having compassion one of another, love as brethren, be pitful, be courteous: ... For the eyes of the Lord are over the righteous, and His ears are open unto their prayers: ..."*

The Japanese wanted to humiliate the Americans to the greatest degree possible. Men with diarrhea, dysentery, upset stomachs or the normal bodily functions were not granted the decency to relieve themselves with a rest stop. I was thankful that none of the illnesses bothered me on the trip. The tight quarters on the train caused you to hope the man next to you would not be bothered with the normal necessities of a rest stop. A runny mess flowed out of the box cars when the doors were opened. The long dusty walk along the treeless road to O'Donnell was a welcome relief from the hot, smelly box cars.

The long columns of four extended ahead of us, as five or six hundred captives walked or at least dragged themselves westward from Capas. Some helped others along the road. The deep breaths of air were the first we had had since morning and they were a great relief to our lungs.

The camp finally came into view and we saw the dilapidated buildings scattered in clusters amid the open spaces. It was originally a Philippine Army training camp before the outbreak of the war. The outstanding thing about the camp was its isolation.

We marched to the eastern gate of the camp near the Japanese headquarters and were herded into an open space to wait in the sun. The small stocky built commandant of the camp took his position on the newly built platform with the formal fanfare of a dignitary. He bellowed his introduction speech to us in no uncertain words as he let us know his hatred of America. He said America and the white race would be destroyed by the Japanese Armed Forces. He thought we were the lowest of the low, in fact he did not recognize us as prisoners of war. He said that we were captives of Japan and were alive because we were the guest of the Emperor. He told us rules would be very strict and immediate death for any attempt to escape. He left no doubt in our minds that he would rather kill us than have the responsibility of our care.

The speech was over and we knew the future was bleak. We were told to spread out so the Japanese guards could divide the captives into sections for an inspection. This inspection was different. Every man and all his possessions were completely searched. We watched to see what items were the center of interest to the guards because occasionally a guard would begin to beat on a man and to yell: bakayoro (fool) or baka (stupid). These were the words used as profanity by the Japanese. We would become very familiar with these two words in the coming years. The men called these terms were slapped and sent to stand in front of the camp commandant. This sent fear through those of us still waiting to be searched.

I remembered the experience on Bataan concerning my New Testament and wondered if they might be looking for Bibles. Finally, the guard stood in front of me. He looked through my field bag, and then asked to see what I had in my pockets. I showed him my New Testament but he did not react unfavorably toward it. I had a few Philippine coins and he looked at each one individually. Finally, to my great relief he told me by sign language to put all my things away.

The men sent in front of the camp commandant were given a very stern and angry lecture in Japanese. A few soldiers took the men over a knoll out of our sight. We heard the sounds of the rifle shots and the guards returned alone. All the men were executed because they had a coin or some curio from Japan. We heard this was done to all the groups as they entered O'Donnell. The commandant assumed that if any American had something made in Japan, it had been taken from a dead Japanese serviceman. This was our first lesson in the dangerous game of trading with the Japanese.

A Major Hazelwood out of the 200th was one of those pulled out of line. He was in our group coming out of Bataan and had traded with a Japanese guard at San Franando for a Japanese coin. This coin was found in the search and it brought death.

The various American outfits were assigned to designated areas. The Filipinos were taken to the west side of O'Donnell. The 200th was given a place which had probably been used by a company or battery of the Philippine Army. These quarters probably seemed fairly roomy to them because they had possibly 125 men in them but the 200th had about 1,200 men come into Camp O'Donnell. We had lost men in the battle, some were sent home on a hospital ship and a few had made it over to Corregidor. The survivors of the march from the

200th were assigned three buildings: two were to be used to quarter the men in the poorest condition and the third building was used for the preparation of food.

I have never heard accurate figures on the number of men who escaped from Bataan to Corregidor, or into the jungles, or even those who died on the march. The reality of the situation was that Camp O'Donnell was a continuation of the march. The full story of the atrocities will never be told, or if told, would not be believed or understood.

The officers were taken away and quartered in another area because the Japanese were very rank conscious. They made almost as much difference between their privates and non-coms, as we make between enlisted men and officers. The work details had enlisted men doing the manual work but the details outside of camp had the officers for supervision. Our detail to Japan had the enlisted men working at three places of employment but the officers had supervisory duty inside the camp compound. I do not recall ever seeing an officer in our area at O'Donnell.

The Japanese did not allow us to visit other areas. Chaplains, as far as I know, were not allowed to visit the men of the various units. This gave me an opportunity to counsel some of the men of my battery and others who knew I was planning on going into the ministry. I had been licensed and planned to be ordained after I finished my seminary training. I read Scriptures and had prayer with some men only a short time before they went into eternity.

Most higher ranked officers including all the generals were taken to Tarlac. The Japanese usually put an American Colonel in charge of the administration of the Americans at the larger camps. The Army's chain of command did not function because the officers were kept in a different place than the men. The Japanese did not want us to be well organized.

Cecil, Bill and I first settled in one of the barracks, but we changed our minds when others came in from the march. The smells from illnesses and the results of the lost control of body functions were nauseous and caused us to retch at the odors. We moved with several other men of our battery to a place that was away from the barracks and latrine.

We were appalled as other men arrived at O'Donnell because each day brought men in poorer health. These men had usually travelled a few more miles. Their feet were swollen, the legs were giving out, the bodies were sagging, the faces were drawn, the eyes sunken into their sockets, and many used their last bit of energy to struggle into the gate at O'Donnell. All were hungry and most were ill with dysentery, diarrhea or malaria. The half rations or less for the past three months had left them in poor physical condition and the march just about finished them off because of the lack of water, food and the atrocities along the way. It was heart breaking to watch men who four months earlier were strong robust specimens of youth, now collapsing from sheer exhaustion.

We talked to each group of new arrivals to obtain information about close friends or other men of our battery. Sometimes we were told that a certain individual had tried to make their way to Corregidor. A good friend of mine had escaped into the jungle to try to live off of the land. Edgar joined the guerillas but was later captured and given the death sentence by the Japanese.

Men gravitated into groups of four to ten men so we could watch out for each other. We had friends in other groups and would help them as strength, energy and circumstances permitted. Even in the groups with men well enough to pull work details, there would be at least one man ill enough to remain in camp and watch the belongings of his group. There was no medicine for the illnesses, so about all we could do for each other was to show some human kindness and compassion. We would try to encourage each other and trust that our situation would improve.

We possessed very little, but every item was precious, including the space we claimed for a place to lay our weary bones at the end of the day. I needed a mess kit at O'Donnell so I took the lining out of my steel helmet. The helmet gave me the desired mess kit until I would be able to locate something more appropriate. The lining gave me a cap for the protection from the hot rays of the sun.

Men with dysentery or diarrhea stayed close to the latrine, but most soiled their clothes without any way to clean them. It was pathetic to watch the deterioration of the human bodies. We did not have anyone with "serious diarrhea" in our immediate group but we had several with malaria. Every day more men moved toward the latrine, as conditions worsened. The death rate was the highest among those who had either diarrhea or dysentery but later malaria caused many deaths. The Japanese were afraid of dysentery and when we were sent to Japan, everyone had to be tested for dysentery before leaving the Philippines. Toward the end of the war, when the Japanese were trying to send all prisoners to Japan they were not screened for dysentery. I learned my first lessons on the disease of malaria here at O'Donnell. A couple of the men in our group had malaria and we watched the progression of the disease. One of the men had the disease with a chill and fever every other day. The lack of medicine caused him to go into the next stage, which was a chill and fever every day. The chills would cause him to shake, so that everything in the near vicinity would tremble. The fever caused increasing temperatures as his whole body seemed aflame. The final stage was cerebral malaria, which meant the chills and fevers would hit him at any time and control of all body functions was gone. He passed away before we left O'Donnell. I had never been ill in the States and medicine seemed to be unimportant, but now I saw the result and necessity of adequate medication to fight tropical diseases. It was very hard to see many friends die because of starvation, illness and diseases when some medicine would have prolonged their life.

The events during the forty-eight days in O'Donnell are the hardest to write because it was a continuation of the "death march". It was a stationary march which ended the struggle for life. Each day was like the previous one, only with fewer alive to ask "Lord, help me make it through the night". Death on Bataan came to a sick, weakened, exhausted prisoner by the point of a bayonet. Death at O'Donnell was almost a welcome relief to a sick, hungry, diseased man. It was a slow agonizing end of the battle of life which had lasted for several weeks.

The typical day started at sunup, unless someone came to me during the night to ask me to go see a friend who needed prayer and the comfort found in the Scriptures. Each morning we found out who had passed away during the night and took them over to a building which served as a morgue. Their deaths were recorded and the corpses were laid on a bamboo swallie in preparation for the funeral detail. I would record any Battery E death in my list of names. We returned to our area where we would be assigned to our detail for the day.

I was probably in about the best health of anyone at O'Donnell. I still had not come down with any of the dreaded diseases and had survived the "death march" in good shape. I knew I would be chosen for a detail every day. There were a few details away from camp and these usually went into Capas or one of the other nearby communities. Every one wanted these details because it gave the person an opportunity to get outside the fence at O'Donnell and to be able to purchase something from the Filipinos. The guards were watching but usually a purchase could be made when the guard was busy somewhere else. I was never on one of these details.

The two main details were grave digging and burial. The grave digging detail went to the north gate of the camp and were issued the shovels. The POWs dug the grave for the day and it was usually a foot or two west of the previous day's grave. The hole was dug fifty feet long by six feet wide and four feet deep. We were always pressed for time to complete the grave in time for the burial detail and were exhausted by the time the grave was completed. The stronger men had to do most of the work because some men were too weak and could barely lift the shovel. Many days we would have the added job of reburial.

The other common detail was the burial detail. If you were placed on this detail, you would pick out three men to work with you. You wanted to find three men who were about your strength. Four men would lay a corpse onto a piece of bamboo swallie about the size of a door with a one inch by four inch board around the outside of the bamboo. The four men must lift together and bring their shoulder under the litter at the same time. If someone failed to lift their share or the timing was not correct then the corpse fell to the ground. Sometimes a man would slip, fall or stumble which might cause all four men to fall. It was increasingly hard to find enough men strong enough to carry the litters on the burial detail. Others daily entered the "too sick to work" group and seldom did a man return to the "well enough to work" group.

This story may seem gruesome to the average reader but it does not go into the details of the unbelievable sights the prisoners of war faced at Camp O'Donnell. The sights of atrocities committed on the "death march", O'Donnell, and aboard the "hell ships" to Japan were sometimes so horrible they are beyond the power of language and description. It is hard to believe a man could treat another man in such an inhuman way. People would have a hard time to understand it unless they had gone through a similar experience. It goes to prove the depravity of mankind and the need of all men for the Savior. The corruption of the human nature allows man to justify himself for treating other people worse than he would treat an animal. Is it any wonder that God in His Word has said the heart of man is deceitful above all things and desperately wicked? We estimated that if the present death rate continued there would be no survivors by Labor Day of 1942. There were about seven thousand Americans who had entered O'Donnell. We were at Camp O'Donnell a little over six weeks and there were over 1,700 deaths. This figures out to be an average of about forty men per day. During this six weeks approximately twenty-five percent of the men who had survived the march died. A record was kept of those in each grave, so that after the war the men laid to rest in O'Donnell and Cabanatuan were moved to a National Cemetery in the city of Manila.

The Japanese asked for volunteers for outside permanent details. These were rumored to be headed for the areas of San Franando or Manila. Some work details tried to salvage things from these areas and on Bataan. I did not like the idea of volunteering for anything and I was pessimistic about the treatment meted out by the Japanese. These details depleted the number of healthy men left at O'Donnell.

I counted some of my best friends among the Navajoes. We had several in our battery and many were in the 200th which was made up of men mostly from the state of New Mexico. Therefore it had native Americans representing several of the tribes. One morning shortly after we arrived at O'Donnell, I was awakened about 3:00 o'clock in the morning. I was asked to come down where the Navajoes had "staked out an area" for themselves. One of them, Johnny, had just passed away and they wanted me to conduct a funeral for him. This was my first funeral service and I counted it a privilege to be able to help them in this time of sorrow.

Johnny was not in my battery, but on our good-will tour of New Mexico it was my privilege to meet him. Cecil and I had gone into an Indian store in Albuquerque and met a couple of the Navajoes from my battery along with Johnny. We admired a beautiful Navajo blanket and we were told the story woven into that blanket. We greatly appreciated hearing the stories of several other blankets and a couple of rugs. Every rug or blanket has a deliberate flaw or error woven into it. The only rug or blanket without a flaw would be one made especially for their chief. I thought this was a wonderful illustration of the perfection of Christ. All of us are like the blankets made with a flaw; we are all sinners. Our chief is the Lord Jesus Christ; and He is the only one without a flaw, He is perfect. Now, my friend Johnny, had gone to meet his heavenly Chief.

The death rate was high for the Native Americans the first few weeks but those who lived past those weeks made it through the rest of the time, unless they were killed in an accident. Several of them helped me a great deal at Cabanatuan. After our return from prison camp one of them was sent with me to Fitzsimmons General Hospital in Denver and he was able to spend several weekends in my home.

Water was scarce and we never had enough of the precious liquid. There was always a long waiting line at the one water faucet which was turned on for a very limited time. We would carry five gallon buckets of water from a creek about a mile away from our area. We were warned not to try to drink the water from the creek because it was contaminated. So we had to carry the water back to boil it in a fifty-five gallon tar drum. The top of the boiled water was siphoned off to get rid of the tar residue. We were lucky to be issued a canteen cup of water per man per day for all purposes. Three of us limited the use of our water very sparingly. We would take about a tablespoon of water to wash our mess kits after each meal. The first one would wash his mess kit, pass the water on to the second man to wash his mess kit before passing it to the third one to wash his mess kit. Someone would come up to us and ask the last one, "Are you going to throw the water away?" We would give it to him for his mess kit. Can you imagine washing the dishes for a family of three with a spoonful of water? I would have to keep my water in my canteen cup, or I would put it into Cecil's or Bill's canteen.

We did everything possible to conserve water. We took a sip and rinsed our mouth before swallowing the water. There were times we would dream of resting beside a cool spring with all the water we could drink. I thought of PSALM 23:2, ". . . He leadeth me beside the still waters." I wonder, when was the last time you thought to thank the Lord for that cup of cool refreshing water, or do you just take it for granted?

The filthy conditions at camp proved to be the ideal breeding place for blow flies. Now I can understand the plague of flies in Egypt during the days of Moses. Our flies were not the common everyday house flies but they were the large blue blow flies. We had swarms of flies which overwhelmed us and they literally fought us for every bite of food. They were bad at all times of the day but they were exceptionally annoying at meal times. Our left hand was kept busy trying to keep the bombing attacks of the flies away from our mess kits as we attempted to reach our mouths with the food before the flies could land upon it. There were times when we wished we had four arms, three of them to drive the flies away and one to hold the spoon. Naturally, the worst times were when the food reached our mouth at the same time as the fly.

The flies, in comparison to other flies, seemed about the size of a bomber, but they dived like a Zero. I do not think I ate an entire meal at O'Donnell without having to remove a few kamikazes from my food. We would have other pests at various times in camp but I do not believe any of them could make a person feel so unclean as the flies. The men who were ill tried to keep the flies off of their bodies but the seriously sick men accepted the fact that the flies were too thick and numerous. The open latrines were full of the flies. We were constantly living in an area that would be considered unsanitary for the beasts of the fields.

We were fighting the flies for food which would not be eaten in the States. Three times a day we received a ration of moldy soupy watery rice. A five gallon bucket of it was supposed to feed one hundred men, or about two-thirds of a cup per person. It was full of weevils but they were our main source of protein. If we had attempted to take out the weevils, we would have been without anything left to eat. The only vegetables we had for food at O'Donnell was gourd soup. It was served with the lugao, but even the flies did not bother the gourd soup. I do not recall any other vegetables during the entire time at O'Donnell.

Occasionally someone on an outside detail would come back with some canned goods or vegetables. The rest of us would watch them with envy and hope we would have the opportunity for an outside detail. Then we could eat something beside the lugao and gourd soup.

Men at O'Donnell shared food with friends but the attitude which developed at Cabanatuan was more selfish. I think some of this was because at O'Donnell we were with men we had known for nearly a year, and some had known each other since childhood. We were scattered among strangers at Cabanatuan and the other camps.

There is a closeness between all the men from Bataan and Corregidor because the experiences at the Japanese prisoner of war camps gave us a mutual love and respect but there is a special bonding of those who survived the march out of Bataan and O'Donnell. Perhaps, it was because fewer of us survived.

Another major problem started at O'Donnell. Some men refused to eat the lugao and would say that they never did like rice, or that this rice was not fit to eat. If we had eaten rice before the war, it was in a pudding with a lot of milk and sugar or it was mixed with meat and vegetables. There could be no argument about the quality, but it was all we had to eat, so we would eat it or plan to die within a few days. Whenever someone came out with the statement that they could not eat anymore lugao, we knew they had basically given up and would be dead within a short time.

When a good friend refused food we would start insulting him. Something was needed to make them angry enough to fight for their life and most of the time it worked. Sometimes the person would get violently angry at us and became determined to show us that they were not a quitter. Our purpose was accomplished because our goal was to make them fight to live. This was another reason for having good friends because all of us at one time or another could have given up. It took a determined effort to stay alive when everything went wrong. We had to make up our minds that the moldy, soupy, watery, wormy lugao was edible. Probably everyone who made it back to the States had to convince himself to keep eating at some time during the three and a half years.

The Americans suffered a great deal but I also felt sorry for the Filipinos. The Japanese theme was, "The orient for the orientals". We were despised but they were considered traitors to their race. We were there to help the Filipinos and they found ways to show appreciation and friendship toward us. Many endangered their lives to give us food and encouragement by flashing the V for Victory sign. It must have been very hard to see the great destruction caused in their land. Manila was reported as the second most destroyed city of the Allies. Families were broken up and many of the civilians were killed during the course of the battle. Homes and lands were deserted with all or most personal possessions lost or stolen.

The fall of Corregidor destroyed all lingering hopes that we still possessed a foothold in the Philippines. We were concerned about the welfare of the men captured there and our friends who had tried to escape from Bataan to the Rock. We did not want them brought to O'Donnell.

Japan's control of land and seas for over a thousand miles in all directions made us aware that our imprisonment would be a long ordeal. America would have to fight back island by island until Japan was defeated. We were still confident the war would be won by the United States and our allies but the question was: How long? The war was on at least two fronts, so the supplies would be divided between Asia and Europe. One of them would probably receive the priority and we could only hope some would come to the Far East. Our questions stemmed from anxiety. Would we be forgotten?

The men who had been in the Philippines for over a year were increasingly concerned about the approach of the rainy season that began in June and lasted through September. Then there would be the month of typhoons, which meant heavy rains with strong winds. If we thought the camp conditions were bad now, just wait until we would experience heavy rains everyday. The ground would become a quagmire in rainy season. The water table was near ground level and certain areas would become a swamp. Some areas of the cemetery had high water in dry season and the problem of giving a decent burial to our fellow prisoners would become a greater task.

We heard many rumors about the Japanese attitude toward prisoners. Most of these were verified by the sadistic actions of our guards. One of the rumors was that General Homma had made the statement that there would be no American survivors from the Philippines. We thought the fulfillment of the rumor was in the near future. It was a happy day for us when we heard General Homma was relieved of his command in the Philippines. Our conditions improved after his dismissal.

Later, I heard the statement of "no American survivors" was actually made by a Colonel Tsuji, who was a staff officer under General Homma. Colonel Tsuji was determined to kill all westerners and put to death any Asian who fought against Japan. He gave orders under Homma's name to put to death all leaders of the Philippines who worked with the United States and this included all American servicemen and the Filipino troops supporting the defense of the Philippines.

Instructions to destroy all Americans reached some of the Japanese troops and commanders but not others. Therefore, the treatment received varied a great deal. The Japanese leaders at O'Donnell followed the orders of Colonel Tsuji. We were weak, sick, and weary with scant provisions, practically no shelter, and we were surrounded by the hostile enemy who ruled with brutal force.

We tried to blot out the reality of our existence and make believe that the events were a nightmare, but reality had a way of returning when we looked around us. The area occupied by the 200th was sloping from the south downward to a low place on the north side. The straddle trench was built near the lowest part of the area. The two barracks were built near the north side of our part of the prison. The sickest men stayed in the barracks or between the barracks and the straddle trench. The men in better shape picked out a spot on higher ground and our group had picked out an area up the hill near a third building.

Practically none of the men in O'Donnell had a blanket and we laid down on the ground in our clothes. There was nothing except dirt under us and nothing to cover us, except the blue sky. There were no pillows to rest our head but some of the men would put their field bag with all of their earthly possessions under their heads which would be uncomfortable but it was easier on their necks.

The filth was worst around the straddle trenches and existence gradually improved the further a person could stay up the slope. No areas were completely free from the results of body functional accidents and there was no water to clean either the ground or individuals. Teeth could not be brushed, the hands and face received no washing, and clothes were worn day and night without any changes. The faces were unshaven. One friend had only a few whiskers and one day he pulled them. Each day conditions became worse and we were helpless to improve them. The odors were beyond description. The commander and the guards were determined to destroy all the Americans under their supervision.

Welcome news was received by the way of a rumor about the last week of May, that a move was in store for us in the near future. We would go to another camp on Luzon where the men captured on Corregidor were being held. We thought any place would be an improvement over O'Donnell. It was the first of June when we received orders to assemble our few earthly possessions for a move.

A few men were left behind but most of us were marched to the railroad station at Capas where we boarded the train for places unknown. The Filipinos gave us the "V for Victory" sign behind the backs of our guards. A string of boxcars waited our arrival. We were not as crowded this time and it was not nearly

52

as hot because the guards allowed the doors of the boxcars to be left open a little. The horrors of O'Donnell had lasted only seven weeks but seemed like a year of misery. The men once again began to have a flicker of hope that some of us would survive the rigors of prison life.

The train headed south toward Manila, so rumors (wishful thinking) that we were to be imprisoned in or near the capitol city of the Philippines were started. We rode through San Fernando but then began to head north and east of Capas. Since the rumors about Manila proved false, someone mentioned that they had heard we were going to a city named Cabanatuan.

The main lessons of O'Donnell can be summed up in the words, "communication" and "compassion". Communications were limited on Bataan but we were completely separated from news of the outside world for the first time at O'Donnell. We appreciated "compassion" in a sense which none of us had ever known before. Compassion was all we could give to others as we watched them deteriorate. Spiritually, we were glad God had communicated with us through the Scriptures. We were able to understand His compassion toward us, "in that while we were yet sinners, Christ died for us". There was nothing we could personally do because of our sins, but we are thankful for the compassion of Christ to meet our spiritual needs by His death for us.

CHAPTER V

CABANATUAN

I CORINTHIANS 10:13, *"There hath no temptation taken you but such as is common to man: but God is faithful and will not suffer you to be tempted above that ye are able: but will with the temptation also make a way to escape, that ye may be able to bear it."*

I PETER 5:7, *"Casting all your care upon Him: for He careth for you."*

Hope springs eternal in the human heart. We always hoped the days in the future would be better than the past or present. The thoughts of spending rainy season in O'Donnell was the worst aspect of a nightmare about to happen. Each day saw our hopes about to be extinguished upon the rocks of despair. Our spirits were kept alive by rumors. Each P.O.W. faced his situation in a little different manner. Therefore, the things remembered or blotted out of the mind varied with each person. The believers were kept going by the promises which are ours in Christ.

It has been stated that there are three main reasons for people to use drugs or alcohol: to blot out the memories of the past, the reality of the present, or the prospects of the future. A similar statement could be made in regards to the depression of the prisoners of war that caused them to quit fighting to live or give up. The past consisted of months of the conflict; and our present involved the realities of our internment camps. Neither of these were refreshing, so we needed to look to the future. The immediate future offered very little, so we had to look beyond "tomorrow" to a distant future. Many times because of serious impairment to physical health, a prisoner could not look much beyond the immediate future. The believers had a bright future with the blessed hope centered in the person of the LORD JESUS CHRIST. Especially where He said, "that where I am, there may ye be also."

P.O.W.s constantly circulated rumors. Some of them had no basic reason, except to raise hopes of a better tomorrow. The best rumor at any time was that we were being traded back to the United States within a few weeks, and that we would head for Australia on the first leg of our repatriation. Naturally, this one always proved false. The worst rumors were that we were expendable and unwanted by the United States, and that the

President's wife had said we were unfit for society. The truth was usually somewhere between the best and the worst but rumors helped sustain our mental health at times of distress. The train finally stopped in the city of Cabanatuan. We were glad the trip was over and we would soon be in our "new home". The area of the city of Cabanatuan did not seem very large but it had a fair size population. The cities in the Philippines have a higher density of population than we have in the States. Cabanatuan is the capitol of Nueva Ecija Province and was about one hundred miles north of Manila. It is on the central Luzon plain, which is the agricultural district of the island. The providential capitol had many government buildings and a good sized business and warehouse district. Several large houses and many smaller homes were on the outskirts of town.

The small towns are called "barrios" in the Philippines. Small homes were built around the landowner's home, a few businesses and the warehouses. The people lived in the barrios but worked their farms which were a few miles away. This is very similar to the Biblical cities, where the people worked their farms but needed the protection of the city walls. Modern warfare has destroyed this concept of city planning.

This area was pleasant to our eyes as we headed east from the city of Cabanatuan toward the hills. We saw a few houses along the road with some Filipinos in their fields with water buffalo. Water buffalo are interesting to watch because they are a stubborn animal and will work until the desire to enter a water pond possesses them.

We appreciated the friendliness of the Filipinos and many of them risked their lives to express a mutual interest in us. Once we were fighting a common enemy and now we were both fighting for our existence. Disease, starvation, and maltreatment by the Japanese were our common bond and we both looked forward to the liberation of the Philippines. Little did I realize I would meet someone from one of these farms later in life.

I spoke about my experiences at a church fellowship meeting in Wisconsin fifteen years after the war. A young Filipino lady was crying and she told me afterward that her family lived almost directly across from the POW camp at Cabanatuan. Her father was imprisoned and her uncle killed for helping the Americans. She was dressed as a boy during the Japanese occupation, because of the treatment given to girls and women. She and her family had come to know Christ over a radio broadcast from Manila. She was in America as an exchange student.

The men in the field hospitals on Bataan were brought to Cabanatuan and the Corregidor prisoners arrived later. Cabanatuan was the merger of three camps. Camp one was finally the headquarters for all the American prisoners in the Philippines. These camps were originally the site of an American agricultural experimental station. They were taken over by the 91st Philippine Army Division for three of their regiments. The barracks had swallie siding and nipa thatched roofs. They were sixty feet by twenty four feet and were built to house forty Filipinos. We housed one hundred men to a barracks on the hospital side of the compound because they were divided into bays (five men side by side and two levels high). The duty side often had over a hundred men to a barracks. There were other buildings in the area that were originally used for a dispensary, garage, office building and a guardhouse.

A bay was the term used to describe the sectioned off areas of large open dormitory type buildings or ship's quarters. Posts were used to hold up the structure and the upper bays were also used to define the enclosed area.

The march of over four miles seemed easier when the mind could think of other things instead of worry about the distance to camp. My first thoughts were concerning adequate housing or would it still be inadequate like O'Donnell? Would sanitary conditions be any better? Would the new camp be suitable for rainy season? Would I ever take a drink of water for granted and think nothing of it? Would I ever forget to thank God for every precious drop of that refreshing liquid? Would we have an increase in our diet? Would I find a blanket and some clothes before rainy season? Would I find a mess kit, canteen and a fork? O'Donnell was finally a memory but not forgotten, and I hoped for a better future. I tried to concentrate on the words of the Apostle Paul, ". . . forgetting those things which are behind, and reaching forth unto those things which are before, I press toward the mark for the prize of the high calling of God in Christ Jesus."

It was a relief when the Cabanatuan camp came into view. We moved past the first set of buildings, which became the hospital area. This area had thirty-one buildings for regular wards and a couple other buildings for isolation wards. There were several kitchens. The doctors would use some for office

56

buildings and some small buildings were used for their quarters. The center area was used for Japanese headquarters. A road divided the Japanese section from the eastern side. The eastern side of the camp was divided into three sections, numerous barracks in each. Cecil, Bill, and I were assigned to the same barracks in the upper end of the second section. We did not have a lot of space but it was shelter.

The men already in the barracks had been captured on Corregidor. We envied their physical condition compared with ours. They had been able to bring personal items, blankets and spare clothing. Their clothes were fairly clean, whereas ours had been worn for two months and we had been unable to even wash them. The entire camp was better organized. The American commanding officer, Marine Colonel Beecher, set up a chain of command and he was an excellent administrator. The officers were quartered in the small office buildings and barracks. The Marines were in the third section of the camp and many of us felt the Marines ended up with a greater percentage of the good details. There was a general tendency of evaluating every detail, action, favoritism or apparent partiality because every grain of food was important to sustain life.

American engineers worked at the mines near the city of Baguio before the war and were inducted into the United States Army. Colonel Beecher assigned them the responsibility for sanitation. They used their knowledge of soils and insisted that a new latrine trench had to be dug before the one in use was unusable. The Japanese had prevented any actions to maintain cleanliness at O'Donnell, so the ground there had been filthy and full of defecation. The P.O.W.s were glad the Colonel had the authority and enough well men to assign the necessary work details to keep the camp cleaner. Small drainage ditches were dug throughout the camp so that excess water could run away from the buildings and pathways. The Japanese officers had a better attitude than the officer at O'Donnell. They permitted the necessary work to allow the camp to be cleaned up.

At first the details on work assignments were primarily used to prepare the camp for our internment. It also included work to make it more convenient for the guards. There were the necessary everyday tasks for running camp including the still-dreaded grave digging and the burial details. A truck load of prisoners cut fire wood for the kitchen to cook the meals. We received some tools to be used in the repair of camp and preparation of camp for the rainy season. Sometimes prisoners were sent to Cabanatuan for the kitchen supplies and certain necessary items. Some details would go into Manila and some of the men with civilian connections in Manila were able to use this group to smuggle letters and contraband into camp.

The work assignments away from camp were the choice details because a prisoner was usually able to buy some things from the Filipinos. At first, these purchases were used by the individual and their friends, but it led to a black market inside camp. Some of us had a few American dollars but a few arrived with large sums of dollars. A person soon learned it was better to have several one dollar bills instead of a large bill.

It became big business to purchase things outside camp and bring into camp for the black market. Almost anything could be purchased inside camp for a price. Rumors stated some of the Japanese guards were in on the action and received their commission. Some prisoners who made a fortune on the black market were among the last to leave the Philippines and died on the hell ships which were sunk.

Main items in the black market were cigarettes. Smokers would trade almost anything for another cigarette and many times it cost them their lives. There was nearly always someone yelling out, "A ration of food for a half of a cigarette". Our ration of food was at starvation level and a person only had to miss a day or two for his body to pass the point of no return. A couple of days of trading food for cigarettes, the man would die.

My assignments for the first six weeks fell into one of three details. I would be called out for the grave digging detail, the burial detail or the Burma road detail.

Some of the land around Cabanatuan camp was marsh land. The guards did not want to walk in the mud, so they decided a guard path should be erected to keep them out of the mud. The prisoners were forced to build a rocky path around the camp and over the marshes. They named the project, "the Burma road project". A rocky creek bottom bisected the camp area a little south of our living quarters. The rocks in the creek bottom were the size of baseballs to the size of footballs. The P.O.W.s were lined up from the creek bottom to the place needed for the path which varied in distance according to the completion of the sections of the path. We would line up five or six feet apart. A rock would be started at the creek and come up the line, man to man, until it arrived at the end of the line where it would be set in place. The guards were spaced about every ten yards and any prisoner who dropped a rock was rewarded with a club blow along the side of his head. Everyone tried to make a good toss to the next man and hoped he would receive a good toss from the man throwing to him. We tried to keep the rocks coming steadily but not too fast to handle correctly. We were glad when this project was completed.

I was still using my steel helmet for a mess kit. My worldly possessions remained the same and I had not received the things I felt were necessities. I had always considered a blanket a necessity but for the year and a half in prison camp in the Philippines I did not have one. The weather was usually warm enough to be without a blanket but there were times when it would have been wonderful to have had a blanket to wrap around a "chilled to the bone" body.

The food improved with a better variety of a few vegetables and once in a great while some meat. Some of the improvements were due to the better kitchen facilities. Each kitchen was organized with an officer for the mess officer, regular cooks and helpers had definite responsibilities. Each kitchen fed several hundred men. The kitchen I ate out of the most was in the upper area of the hospital side and it fed five barracks of one hundred men each. The cooks learned how to cook the rice. The first rice was called lugao which was a mush but later the rice was steamed. The rice was a better quality than at O'Donnell.

Cabanatuan had a sufficient water supply for our drinking and cooking purposes. Our first showers were taken in the month of June and it was a great blessing to clean our bodies. Rainy season began in June and the first few days we could almost set our watches by the time of the rain clouds. We laughed at the men captured on Corregidor who had brought soap in their personal things. It was funny to see them get all lathered up, and then have the rain showers ceased. We knew the showers were gone until the next day. We were able to take all the baths we desired during rainy season but during the dry season they were limited.

The evil, sinful nature of man was demonstrated in many ways. Former close friends sometimes became very selfish if one of them was in one of the cliques. They would not help others but demanded an outrageous price for something a former friend needed to sustain life. There were times we would give any thing we had to purchase certain medicines and fruit. Many men did make it back to the States because they had a friend at all times of need. Someone who was willing to risk their own life for their friend.

I know I would not have survived had it not been for several close friends who went beyond the call of duty to see that I was provided with absolute necessities when in serious need. I also believe there were others who made it back because I was able to help them in their times of greatest need. True friends were more precious than gold. As a believer, I believe these friends were provided for me in the providence of God. I firmly believe there are no accidents in the life of the child of God. We do not have good or bad luck but we can rely upon the providence of God. It is wonderful how the Lord always had the right person in the right place at the right time. He has promised never to leave us or to forsake us.

"Why didn't you try to escape?" is a standard question asked POWs. I am sure this thought entered the mind of every P.O.W at some time during his incarceration. There are several factors in the answer of the question. The opportunity of escape is not always present. The place for an escape is important. An American sticks out as different from the vast majority of the natives in the Orient. Protecting cover had to be available which would include the possibility of blending into the natural surroundings as well as with natives. If we could have escaped into the jungle, we would have had the natural cover and the Filipinos would have helped us. The percentage factor must be given consideration; the possibility for the individual making it and the consideration for those left behind. The last named reason was our greatest concern.

The Japanese divided us into groups of ten men. If one man escaped, the other nine had to dig their own graves and were shot. If all ten of the men of a group made a mass escape, then nine other groups were taken out and executed. The Japanese made it clear that for every man who escaped or attempted to escape, the lives of nine men would be taken by a firing squad.

We had several examples of the principle of nine for one. Soon after we arrived at Cabanatuan several men were caught going through the fence. They were going out to buy some things on the outside and bring them back to camp. The Japanese called all of us out and made us watch the men dig their graves. They were forced to kneel behind the hole and a firing squad shot them. Their final act was to fall into the hole they had dug for themselves. It was very gruesome to watch.

It was immediately after this event that the Japanese told us that the nine for one rule was in effect.

One day a man disappeared from his detail. The Japanese came into camp and took the remaining nine men. We were concerned and worried because we were certain that nine men would be killed. My good friend, Jesse Miller, was in this man's group. The Japanese did not let us have any personal contact with them but said they would be shot the following day. Several of us spent much time in prayer that the Lord would see fit to spare their lives. We knew the Lord could protect the life of His child as long as His child's work in this life was still unfinished. The Japanese announced an almost hour by hour delay. The tension mounted for several days, as the Japanese made postponements. Each postponement encouraged our hearts that their lives would be spared. Finally the men were allowed to return to their barracks. It was a time of great rejoicing to the Lord for answered prayer and His protection.

Cecil became ill around the first of July. His illness was considered serious enough to be sent to the so-called hospital. I went over to the hospital several times in the next week or ten days on burial details. The morgue was located near the center of the hospital area and the burial detail went to the morgue. I was unable to find out how Cecil was doing or learn anything about where he was quartered or if his health was improving.

The burial details were similar to the ones used at O'Donnell. The corpse was placed upon the bamboo swallie. Four men worked together to pick up the corners of the litter and lift it upon their shoulders. We marched about a half mile to the cemetery. Everything went fine as long as each one kept in step and walked in unison. We had a common courtesy that if we needed to stop, turn to the right or left, we would tell the other three men of our litter bearing group.

One day, during the second week of July 1942, something happened that greatly changed my life. Rain had fallen the night before and water was standing or running in a number of places. We would walk through water a few inches deep and step over areas under three feet wide. I went to the morgue on a burial detail where three men asked me to work with them on a litter. I took the left front corner of the litter and all was fine until we came to a little ditch near the cemetery. It was about thirty inches wide, so I said I was planning to step across it and they all agreed. I stepped across but the other three men stopped. My foot gave away and I lost my balance. I fell to the ground which caused my side of the litter to drop. The corpse fell on top of me and I came face to face with the dead man. I was very disgusted and they all said that they had suddenly decided not to take a chance of getting their feet wet. Almost every other group had stepped across but I happened to be in the one group which changed their minds. I was a soaking wet prisoner who wished for a blanket, so I could take my clothes off during the night instead of sleeping in them. The man had died of diphtheria, a disease which I had heard about but knew little about it.

A couple of days later, I had a sore throat and reported to the Medics. I thought it was caused by being wet and not able to dry my clothes. The Medics took one look at my throat and yelled for me to go stand by myself. Finally, the sickest were taken across the center section of camp to the hospital. Some men had to be carried and some were able to walk over on their own power, but a couple of us had to walk a few yards at the rear of the line.

The other men were taken to the various wards but the two of us were told to go to isolation ward 00. My friend Cecil saw me, when I walked past. He asked me where I was going and I told him to double 0. This was the ward for those with the dreaded disease, diphtheria. There were two isolation wards; 0 for those with amoebic dysentery and 00 for those with diphtheria. The life expectancy for those in 0 was a couple of days and the ones in 00 usually died the next night. No one was expected to survive from either of these wards, but especially no one was expected to walk out of 00.

Cecil had recovered from his illness and was on a detail to cut fire wood for the kitchen in the lower area of the hospital. He would come within a short distance from the fence around ward 00 and he would encourage me in my fight against the disease.

The ward doctor stood about twenty feet away from me and told me to open my mouth as wide as possible, but not to breath in his direction. He sent me to a large room about twenty feet square. There were at least twenty men in the room and I added my few belongings to the floor area.

Our doctor made his rounds every morning. He would yell at us from the gate and tell us to get to the far side of the room for a lineup. He would stand at the door and ask us how we were feeling. We would answer his questions about our throats, our eating problems, and if we were feeling weaker than the previous day. The doctor would apologize that he did not have any anti-toxin to give us. We never did receive any anti-toxin to fight diphtheria. Death from diphtheria was a death by strangulation because the throat would close. In all due fairness to the doctor, he was a surgeon and he performed some great operations which saved many lives. No doctor could help us in "dip ward", without a drop of medicine to give relief for our throats. It was very depressing to realize that we were considered outcasts and rejected by our fellow men.

The two isolation wards were enclosed by a fence. A kitchen helper brought our food to the gate in a five gallon bucket. If any of us were standing close to the fence, we were told to get completely away until after the food was set inside the area and the helper returned to safety. I learned how a leper must have felt in Biblical times when they had to cry out, "Unclean, unclean". It is depressing to have to keep your distance from other people.

It is almost impossible to swallow with diphtheria and it would take us a long time to finish our food, but some men found it was impossible to swallow any food. We would complete our meal, and one of us would take the container over to the gate. Someone would take the container to the kitchen where the bucket was scalded so it would be ready for us at the next meal. Our rations were cut, so that no food would be wasted.

Days and nights were long because there was no relief for the sore throats. Men with diphtheria were basically waiting for death which occurred within a few days but many times within the first twenty four hours. Death came from either choking to death or from starvation or by a combination of the two.

Whenever anyone died in "dip ward", the strongest patients carried the corpse to the gate. We would place it on a bamboo swallie litter so the litter bearers would not have any personal contact with the victim of diphtheria. This kept any person without diphtheria from having to enter the buildings or the area of 00 ward.

There were between 125 to 150 men who contacted diphtheria at Cabanatuan. I know of only five of us who left ward 00 to return to the regular hospital area. I think three of these men are dead and the other one I have not heard from since I left the Philippines for Japan. Once, I heard that he made it through the prison camps and returned to the States. I heard later of another man who lived through diphtheria.

63

The administrative policy at Cabanatuan was to take an inventory of personal property which hindered stealing of necessary items. Most of the time when a man came to ward 00, all except the clothes he was wearing and mess equipment were taken away because he was not expected to return to claim his personal belongings. The first opportunity to obtain a dead man's cup, mess kit, cup, fork, spoon, knife and canteen were given to those in his same barracks. I was able to get a mess kit, cup, fork, spoon, knife and canteen through the system.

When we inherited a metal utensil used for food or water, we wanted them to be clean. We washed them in water and scrubbed them with sand. We had plenty of time to make the metal shine as if it had been polished with sandpaper. We used our G.I. knives to engrave our names or whatever we wanted into the metal containers, especially our canteens. Some canteens were works of art.

The reason for the engraving was that these utensils had a tendency of disappearing when a person became incapacitated. If the name was engraved into the metal, it gave a positive identification of ownership. I carved my name on the acquired property so that my proof was beyond question. I scratched all of my organizations and camps on the canteen and brought it home after the war. It is one of my souvenirs that I retained to remind me of our Lord's watchcare.

The worst time for me with diphtheria was in the first few days when the membrane of my throat closed. Gradually, it began to clear up and the soreness left my throat. My strength improved and I had hopes of being one of the few who would ever walk out of this ward. Five of us were moved into a vacant room next to the gate where we were used as a buffer group. We were assigned the job of receiving the food, dishing it out into the patients mess kits, and carrying corpses to the litters. The doctors retained us in the area longer than usual because they did not want to take any chance of us being a carrier of the dreaded disease.

Diphtheria was brought under control and when no new cases developed for a couple of weeks, the doctor told us that we had been under quarantine long enough to recover from the disease which had taken many lives throughout history. He checked us to make sure that we were not carriers and told us that he was glad we were able to recover under such conditions, but that he never thought any of us would live. The five of us had lived through one of the most dreaded diseases, in spite of poor conditions, poor housing, little food and no medicine to alleviate the soreness in our throats. The doctor warned us that our problems were not finished but to expect paralysis that could affect any part of our bodies. Paralysis attacks would probably affect our throats, legs and arms.

We moved from one end of the hospital area to the opposite end to our new "home", Ward 30. It was a ward for men who were partly recovered from a variety of diseases. Our welcome was very unique — about like a group of paupers showing up at an exclusive luxury hotel. Only, we had to be accepted. No one wanted to share a building, let alone sleep next to someone who had had diphtheria. Lieutenant Hardegree was in charge of Ward 30, and he made a hard decision. He solved his dilemma by moving all the officers into the first upper bay on the left of the barracks and moved all the enlisted men into vacant places throughout the building. The five of us were assigned to the lower left bay and we had found a new beginning.

The bottom bays were about five feet in height but the upper bays were high enough in the center for a person to stand up. The center aisle was about five feet wide and each bay was about sixteen feet long by seven feet deep. Each barracks had space for a hundred men with five men in each bay, even though the Filipinos had originally assigned forty men per barracks. The bays were covered with strips of bamboo a couple of inches wide with a space between the strips. The sides of the barracks were made out of bamboo swallie with a series of large windows. There were no doors on the building, only an open space. The large windows and open spaces were to protect the building in the case of a typhoon.

Every morning we checked to see who lived through the night. Death rates were less than a few months earlier, but we lost a man out of our barracks every few days. We lost about one a week from our barracks the later part of 1942. It was a wonderful day early in 1943 when no POW died that day. By the time I left for Japan, over 2600 men had died at Cabanatuan.

The prisoners had many arguments about every subject. Most of them were good natured and the men remained friendly but occasionally it ended in a fight. I think the worst one happened while I was in dip ward where two men in 0 ward got into an argument and soon became angry. Both men were close to death because of amoebic dysentery and neither could lift himself up. One held a full canteen of water over his opponent's head and dropped it. They kept dropping the canteen on the other person's head until their energy was gone. No one in the ward was well enough to stop the fight. Both men died before the end of the day. The depravity of the human nature always reveals itself to show the necessity of salvation which can only be provided by faith in the Lord Jesus Christ.

We were given a small bowl of rice and some kind of soup each day. I have eaten almost every kind of vegetable tops boiled and served as soup. A soup made out of komotes (sweet potatoes) would have tasted better if served raw because we could have spit out the rotten parts. We did not receive enough fruits and vegetables to get the proper vitamins and especially vitamin C. I have eaten the following animals in the Philippines: mules, horses, monkeys, dogs, and occasionally an iguana or other kind of lizard which fell into the cooking vats. Those little pieces of meat helped to improve our diet.

The administration had made improvements in sanitation and cleanliness. We used straddle trenches for latrines, and they are not known for being conducive for pleasant conditions. An open trench is uncomfortable and a breeding place for filth. Occasionally a sick man would fall into the open trench or a person's foot might slip and cause him to fall into the crawling corruption. It was a mess to clean up after such a tragic misstep. The changing weather conditions also caused a variety of problems.

Many of us never had any personal toilet articles; such as a bar of soap, a toothbrush or a comb. If we were able to take a bath, we were dried by the sun. The Japanese issued us one article of clothing. It was a piece of cloth ten inches wide by thirty inches long with a string across one end. The string was wrapped around the body. The cloth was draped around the lower part of the body and tucked through the string. This loin cloth covered the private parts of the men, and it was all right in an all male camp. This gave us a covering, especially after our uniforms wore out. The patches on my trousers had patches upon the patches.

Several pests swept through camp and affected every person regardless of their own personal habits. The first plague to sweep Cabanatuan was the grey-back lice which were probably brought in by one of the returning details. It was not long until everyone in camp was infected with them. The only way to combat the menace was to take off your clothes, pick out the lice and eggs from the seams of your garments and pop them with the fingernails. This would allow a little peace and if done near nightfall allowed a good night sleep. Later, large barrels of boiling water were set up, and the men would bring their clothes and put them into the barrel. It defeated the lice.

The next menace to plague camp was the bed-bug. They were everywhere and were a greater menace than the lice. They could not be killed by smashing them between the fingernails. Squashing them also left a very unpleasant odor. Someone got the bright idea that the bays could be taken outside and placed on an ant hill for the day. The ants had a feast and the P.O.W.s were able to sleep better for a few days. The five of us who had come from diphtheria ward protested having to take our bay outside to the ant hill. We had the only bay without bed bugs because something in our blood caused by the disease must have been repulsive to the bugs. We were glad the bugs thought we were undesirables. The ward officer was willing to look at our bay and sure enough there were no bugs! He accepted our proof and granted us the right not to take our bay outside. It was hard work to maneuver the bays outside, and this was the only time the other prisoners envied us for having diphtheria.

If there was a menace of pests in one camp it was not long until it spread to the other camps. Men healthy enough to go out on a work detail were sent from Cabanatuan to reinforce the work groups and sick men returned to Cabanatuan. Japan had an abundance of very fast moving sand fleas. The other pests did not give me much of a problem but the fleas were a nadir of misery. If a flea got on my foot and started up my leg, by the time I killed it there was a row of welts from my toe to my thigh.

We wanted to go back to the duty side of camp because the workers received larger rations. The diphtheria survivors were warned not to return to duty until there was an absence of a paralysis attack for at least six weeks. I had an attack of paralysis every few weeks for the first five months after my recovery. My arms would be partly paralyzed to the degree that I had a hard time holding anything in my hands. My legs refused to go forward more than a shuffle. A foot-wide drainage ditch in front of our barracks had a bridge built across it. I could not step across the ditch, so I would have to shuffle across at the bridge.

One time my throat was partly paralyzed for seven days and completely paralyzed for three days. I had a hard time with food and water for the seven days, but for three days every bite of food or drink of water came back out of my nose. It was a very eerie feeling and certainly a relief when my throat reopened. The worst time I had was shortly before Christmas 1942. I had a heart attack caused by diphtheritic paralysis. I was in a coma for seventeen days and those days were completely blotted out of my mind. The heart attack was my last paralysis attack. I had suffered less from the disease, but I had more and harder paralysis attacks than the other four men. I had to learn to walk again after the last and most serious paralysis.

When I returned to the States, I told the doctors at Fitzsimmons General Hospital about the coma. I was told it was impossible for someone to live that long in a coma caused by a diphtheritic paralysis heart attack. The doctors would not record this in my permanent file. Unfortunately, my ward doctor, Dr. Swanson died when one of the POW hell ships was sunk, so I could not get a statement from him.

Dr. Swanson was a great doctor and the Lord used him to help me survive during the first quarter of 1943. He told me that he thought the reason I survived several illnesses was because I had never smoked or drank, and that God had given me an excellent physical body. The "dip" survivors helped one another and we had a close relationship, because we could sympathize with each other on our aches and pains. I met Louis Barry the first day I entered the diphtheria ward, and we slept next to each other for about a year. We helped each other because when one of us had a paralysis attack the other one was feeling fairly well. During the time I was in the coma, Barry would go over to get my food. He said I would raise up and make every effort to swallow as much food as possible. He told me this was the only time I would attempt to move, and I never spoke a word for the entire seventeen days.

The Japanese allowed a little medicine into camp the day I regained consciousness. Dr. Swanson brought me several different kinds of medicine which lasted for three days. This was the first time medicine was permitted to come into camp. The Lord being my Great Physician, it was enough to start me back on the road to recovery. It was about a quarter of a mile to the scale and when I was strong enough to walk I weighed myself. I weighed 102 pounds but at my worst it was probably about 95 pounds. When I played sports in college my playing weight was between 190 to 195 pounds. Thus, you can see that I was just about half of my normal weight.

During the time of my coma, the officer above me had a case of scabbies. He was a great pilot with an excellent combat record but he was a very inconsiderate person. He picked his scabs and dropped them through the bamboo slats onto me. He probably figured I would die anyway, so what difference would it make if I had his scabbies. Fortunately, there was some purple medicine to fight these mites which lay their eggs under the skin, but I had to walk a quarter of a mile to the building where my scabbies could be treated.

I was one of the last to come down with malaria. I had such strong chills that I shook the entire building. After a little time of peace, the fever rose and my temperature soared to 107 1/2 degrees. The barracks officer, who slept in the bay above me, did not want me to mess up the barracks when I died, so he gave instructions to take me outside. The Lord again overruled in the hearts of the Japanese because they permitted a small amount of quinine tablets to be brought into camp. Dr. Swanson was able to get about a dozen for me. The malaria subsided and the Lord brought me back into strength.

Medical terminology distinguishes between the two kinds of beri-beri. The wet beri-beri is caused by the retention of liquids in the body. Some men died from the shock when the liquids were suddenly released. A friend was large one night but he was skin and bones in the morning and he died before noon from the shock. The dry beri-beri was also known as the disease of the burning feet. The feet felt like they were on fire and many men sat on the edge of their bay rubbing their feet. I still make sure my feet are uncovered for at least part of the night. Recently I was at a reunion of the survivors of Bataan and Corregidor and talked to a prison camp doctor who told me my complaint was a common one for those of us who had dry beri-beri.

I did have many diseases at Cabanatuan which were common to all POWs in the Philippines. Everyone had malnutrition, scurvy and pellagra which were caused by deficiencies in vitamins. We all had diarrhea, bruises, cuts, toothaches and skin discomforts. I had yellow jaundice and my skin had a yellow color for many years. Dengue fever is one of the most miserable diseases because every joint in the body hurts and sometimes even the veins ache. I also had several boils and other things too numerous to mention.

We developed a special kind of friendship based upon an understanding of the pressures of prison life. We realized how the other person was suffering, and we could have a compassion and sympathy not normally known by others. We were able to analyze the actions of men under great pressure and some men broke under tension by becoming selfish. Other men showed great character by showing concern and a willingness to help others. We were together twenty-four hours a day and saw their reactions under many different kinds of circumstances. I noticed the order of a child in a family made some differences among the men of my acquaintance. It is only natural that there were many exceptions to my general analysis, but the oldest child in the family seemed to be able to stand up better under the pressures of prison camp. The only child and the baby of the family did not seem to fare as well under the tensions of survival. It appeared to me that the oldest child of a family was accustomed to making decisions and could cope better under the stresses. The only child and baby of the family had decisions made for them, so did not accept the stresses as well.

Death was a constant companion. There was a strong possibility that we might not awaken the next morning, and one of our hardest battles was to never allow ourselves to give up, which would have been easy. Many times I have seen a man who looked in fairly good health make the statement, "I'll never make it back to the States". He would usually be dead by the next morning.

We were given only enough food to sustain life if the person was determined to live. We had to retain "the will to live" because there were more than enough dangers from diseases and accidents. Everyone had their method to cope with their problems, but the main asset was hope. As a believer, I looked forward to a hope anchored in the Lord Jesus Christ.

Attitude was very important and this included his personal attitude and that of others near him. The doctors' attitudes were their main medicine because they were without even common household remedies. They tried to encourage their patients by suggesting the Japanese might release some medicine, or maybe some citrus fruits would be brought into camp to ease the pains and discomforts of scurvy and pellegra. The doctors had an extremely difficult task with so many patients but without the simplest medicines. Most doctors functioned well in the environment and showed concern, consideration and compassion. I did become angry at one doctor when a friend went into a coma and I went for the doctor. It was in the afternoon and I asked for his help, either to come to the ward or tell me what I could do to help my friend. He refused to help until sick call the next morning.

Men reacted to internment in the same ways people react to any other tragic situation in their lives. First, was the denial that this experience was happening to them. A few men tried to go into a shell and blot out the events of each day. Some ex-prisoners of war do not remember much of their experiences because they tried to forget it happened. This was basically a denial.

The next step was bitterness over being prisoners. The anger and bitterness was taken out against God, as though He was the cause of their capture by the Japanese. The bitterness continued after liberation and some until the present time. Many of these men have tried to drown the bitterness under a blanket of alcohol.

Many P.O.W.s returned home with great bitterness toward some things done by another prisoner but mostly toward the Japanese. The guards would slap, beat, or abuse us for no known reason. We were unable to defend ourselves, or even receive a logical reason for their actions. If we lifted a finger to protect ourselves, we would in most cases have been killed on the spot. It is very hard to receive such treatment without becoming bitter. When bitterness has been carried for a long time, it is almost impossible to forgive. I have tried not to carry any bitterness because it would hurt me the most. This may be one of the reasons that I have not had nightmares of the experiences.

We eventually had to accept the reality of our experience and try to make the most out of it. Our lives had to be turned over to the Lord for His strength and abiding comfort. His grace was sufficient to sustain us in the most trying hour. There was no middle ground; either a man wanted to know God and His eternal Word or they refused to have anything to do with Him. No one tried to straddle the fence on spiritual things.

Major Reardon was able to come over to the hospital area quite often and give me information about the other men. He helped me to keep the death record of our Battery roster. I would often receive a message that one of the men wanted to see me. We would talk, read Scripture and have prayer together. Several times we both knew it was a time of parting

71

and our next meeting would be at the feet of Christ. This is the believer's comfort that death to the child of God is "absence from the body and present with the Lord". Usually we would go over the plan of salvation again just to make sure their faith was in the security of the Lord Jesus Christ.

Several men asked me to contact their families after I returned to the States. We gave our addresses to friends and we made an agreement that we would contact the other person's family if we made it back home. Most of the families were gracious and definitely appreciated my visit with them. I knew some of the calls would be hard. I was very thankful, and greatly appreciated several friends who contacted my mother. I became friends with several of the families and we corresponded for a number of years with them.

My mother was always happy for any information about our situation. She was glad for the mother groups which were formed during the war to disperse information about prisoners or those missing in action. A mothers group in New Mexico did a lot of work to inform the families about the 200th.

We did not receive much correspondence. My father passed away about a year after I was captured and I did not find out about his death until after I returned to the United States. I received about a half a dozen letters during the three and a half years as a prisoner of war. My mother wrote at least once a week for the entire time, and I received about 2 per cent of her letters. Other friends wrote and I never received their letters. We did not receive a great deal of information because the writers knew the letters would receive a double censor: American and Japanese.

I was able to write five post cards. These were form cards, which had a few boxes to be checked. The cards looked something like the following:

I am doing — excellent;   good;   fair;   poor
I am feeling — excellent;   good;   fair;   poor
My health is — excellent;   good;   fair;   poor
Give my best regards to:

I would try to fill the card so that my family would know I was thinking clearly. I would put a familiar name so they would realize I had filled out the card. The first card was filled out by Barry who signed my name, while I was in the coma. He found my home address and turned in my card to be mailed. My mother was happy to see the signature and thought it was mine.

It took the card eight months to arrive in Denver. My mother informed the government that she had heard from me. A couple of months later she received a letter from the defense department that someone (my mother) had heard from me and that I was no longer considered missing in action but a prisoner of war.

Barry survived the years in prison camps and wrote to me after the war. I took his letter to my mother and showed her the way he wrote my name. I took the first card written by Barry and a copy of my signature. All three looked alike because Barry signed my signature exactly like I did. I do not think it was an accident that both signed it the same. Again, I think it was the hand of God in providing someone to sign that first card for me.

After I returned to duty, my first detail was to chop wood in the hills east of Cabanatuan. Sam Nez from my battery and I were assigned an axe. I was completely exhausted after a few minutes and Sam would chop for about an hour. This rotation continued for the three or four days I was on this detail. Sam insisted on doing a lion's share of the work. Sam was concerned about my health and insisted that I rest beside a little stream. I thought of the verse in the PSALM, "He maketh me to lie down in green pastures. He leadeth me beside the still waters." Sam Nez had a heart of kindness, consideration and brought to my memory the story of the good Samaritan in LUKE 10:30-37.

The main detail at Cabanatuan camp was the farm. I was in the hospital when the farm program was started. An American POW had been in the Philippines for many years and was familiar with the preparation of the land. All the work was done by hand with few tools and no machinery. There was great variation in the land with some ant hills seven feet tall. The men were divided into three groups. The first group were given picks and were to break the ground. The second group were given hoes to break clods. The third group were given rakes to smooth out the ground. Each individual man was responsible for a space of ground about three and a half feet wide. The main thing to remember was to keep in a straight line. Any man who fell behind in his line was beaten, so it was necessary not to get ahead or behind.

Some ground was always in preparation for a crop. I was

assigned to the preparation and planting of the rice paddies. The paddies were flooded with several inches of water. The young plants had been started elsewhere and were lined up on the edge of the dike between the paddies. Each planter was responsible for a three foot wide space across the paddy. The whole day was spent in bending over planting the young plants. The danger facing us was the rice snake which was about the size and shape of an angleworm but very poisonous. I never knew when any rice snakes were near me so I gave great respect to anything that looked like an angleworm.

Certain sections of the farm were set aside for the various vegetables. We were assigned certain details for all day. The watering detail was spent in carrying five gallon buckets of water to the plants. Each plant was to receive a small amount of water and when one carrier was finished with his bucket of water then the next carrier started with the next plant. Days were spent bending over the plants pulling the weeds. The produce was harvested and placed on a large litter that was carried into camp by groups of eight men. Sometimes a guard would decide to ride on the litter into camp. The extra weight added pain to the barefooted carriers and especially if dry beri-beri was already causing them to hurt. All details had dangers and there was always the possibility of being hit with a club.

The scariest detail on the farm was unassigned. A guard would take some men with shovels and a piece of rope with him to a giant ant hill. The ants hibernated during rainy season. We would have to dig a trench several inches wide and about six inches deep from the top to the bottom of the ant hill. When we found a hibernating cobra snake, one of us would have to take the rope and place it around the snake. Then we would dig the length of the snake and pull it out into the open. Those with shovels stood ready to kill the cobra. Several times I have watched the cobra put out its hood, rise up and strike. I never saw anyone hit by a snake but have seen some near misses. The guard would smile and feast on snake steak for dinner.

We liked to have something special on certain days, such as our birthdays, Christmas and other special days. Cecil, Moore and I would try to get something extra while we were in the Philippines. Wendell Bates was included on these special days in Japan. A highlight of these special times was in the summer of 1943. My birthday fell on a Friday and Moore's was the next Sunday. The Japanese did not give us many days off; in fact, sometimes we worked for three weeks straight before a day off.

The Japanese had told us that we would have Friday off which would be on my birthday. We did not have anything extra for a celebration until two days before the scheduled rest day.

A family friend, Lieutenant Colonel Jack Cook, left a message for me to come to his barracks. I could not imagine why he would send me an urgent message. I walked down to his barracks and knocked on the door. He said, "Leonard, I believe you have a birthday coming up soon, do you not?" "Yes, Sir, I have one this Friday." I replied.

He gave me some food items which he was able to have smuggled in from the outside or more exact from the black market. I was certainly grateful for this answer to prayer and to Colonel Cook. I told Cecil and Moore that we had the ingredients for a birthday cake.

We had soaked the rice during the day and spent Thursday evening grinding our flour. We ground our flour by the "armstrong" method. I will try to describe this method. We found a round bottle and a flat board about the size of a cutting board. We laid the rice on the board and took turns rolling the bottle over the rice, until we were satisfied with the texture of the flour. We had received a coconut and were able to bake it in the kitchen on Thursday evening. We were all set for the next morning.

The Japanese called us out on Friday morning and informed us that we would have to work but would have Sunday off. Can you imagine the musty condition of the flour after two days of moisture? We took my steel helmet which was now used for a water basin when we took a bath. It was a pretty good mixing bowl. We added a mouldy coconut to our musty rice, included an overripe pineapple and two duck eggs. The duck eggs were not exactly fresh but the ducks were not hatched out, even though they were getting fairly close. When Moore looked at the batter he remembered a friend in another barracks who had a couple of bicarbonate of soda tablets. We added them to our batter and it made our cake rise — a little. We mixed a handful of mashed peanuts with a couple of very black skinned bananas for our frosting. This cake certainly tasted good and we thanked the Lord for His provisions. We ate our special birthday cake and thought of the verse, "Thou prepareth a table before me in the presence of mine enemies."

One of my best memories of special food was the time I was recovering from my paralysis attack. The doctors received some canned milk. A small group of men whose illness could be helped by milk was selected to receive it. A friend, Tony James, was in the group chosen. He told me he was allergic to milk so he gave the milk to me. The milk was a great help to me and I am sure it was another in a series of things used to help me recover.

Our guards had all kinds of personalities but the majority had a sadistic nature. There were three main classes of Japanese guards in the Philippines. The battle scarred veterans who seemed to hate their enemies and used any thing to gain vengeance. The young guards from Japan were bucking for acceptance by the veterans. The guards recruited in Furmosa were not trusted by the Japanese. They were considered a little better than us and they received comfort by taking out their agitation on the Americans. We never knew what to expect from the guards. Sometimes they would start out fairly nice to us and for no reason they would suddenly change their attitude.

One of the hardest things for me to witness was the death of a man from Battery E. He was on inside guard duty in the upper area of the hospital. I never understood the reason Americans were on inside guard duty but early one morning, the Japanese officer of the day came upon the American guard at the fence talking with a Japanese guard. We figured the Japanese guard saw he was caught not walking his post in a military manner, and he yelled an American was attempting to escape. The Japanese officer and guard pulled the American through the fence. We were awakened when the three walked past our ward on the way to the guard house just outside the southwest corner of the hospital area. There were usually eight to ten soldiers resting there between tours of guard duty. The guards beat the prisoner with rifle butts every few minutes. At the changing of the guards, all of them would hit him with their rifles. The cry of pain and agony was awful. We actually wished for an immediate death, but they took about three hours to beat him to death. I saw others beat to death, but it is harder to see someone you know killed to satisfy a sadistic nature.

The Japanese guards would sometimes call a person over to the fence. It was a good idea not to get too close to the fence but stay back and talk. It was one of those hard decisions because we had to obey the Japanese, but we had to defend ourselves from being pulled through the fence and be accused of trying to escape. The Japanese guards certainly enjoyed their authority over us. They liked to put us in a situation whereby they could humiliate us.

We picked nick-names for our guards which we felt suited their character, vices, voices, actions, or their sadistic nature. If we found something of merit in a guard, then we gave them a name to reveal the idea. Some of the names were Speedo, Big Speedo, B-17, Air Raid, Hikko, Pop, the Old Man, Henry, Holy Joe, and some names not complimentary. Donald Duck was one of the comic names given to a guard. He received his name because when he was excited, he really sounded like a duck quacking. He asked us the meaning of his name and we informed him that in America everybody knew Donald Duck. He was an important movie star and pictures of him appeared in some daily newspapers After that, whenever he was called by the name, he would feel very important and really strutted.

We were allowed to have group meetings and the chaplains were allowed to function as ministers. The chaplains did wonderful work in Cabanatuan. Many men came to trust the Lord Jesus Christ as their personal Savior, and Chaplain Robert Taylor had an exceptionally good ministry in the hospital area. A recreational officer obtained some musical instruments and a band was formed. The officer worked with men who were interested in being entertainers. We had a variety of programs which helped the attitude throughout camp. There were concerts, talent shows, original plays, comedy, choirs, and occasionally the Japanese would bring in a captured American film. After I left for Japan, I heard about a Disney film brought into camp and shown one night. It was about a comic character named, Donald Duck. One Japanese guard watching the show did not appreciate the film. He spent several days trying to remember who had called him Donald Duck. Needless to say, one guard lost his nickname, or at least to his face.

My barracks on the duty side at Cabanatuan was directly across the road from the Japanese quarters. A guard came out of his barracks one evening with a knife in his hands. He yelled something in Japanese, but we could not understand his statement. He took the knife and while we watched he committed hara kiri.

The reputations of the guards on some of the other details were well known. We had heard about the reputation of the White Angel and the number of deaths he caused. Other guards were known for their cruelty to prisoners. The outside details had an advantage over O'Donnell and Cabanatuan at first but later they became more brutal. The majority of details in 1942 were to clean up the results of the Japanese invasion. The war changed in 1943 and the Japanese were using the POWs to build airfields. They wanted these completed as fast as possible, and the deaths of prisoners were immaterial. The prisoners were driven to complete a field in the shortest time possible and many died. The POWs did find ways to delay the work projects. The outside details grew harder and the reports on them were less favorable. Some of the men were anxious to get away from Cabanatuan, but conditions on work details were unknown.

Cabanatuan was the main prison camp in Luzon, Bilibid was used by the dock detail in Manila and civilians along with the nurses were at Santo Tomas.

Courage, loyalty, and character cannot be bought but they constitute the basic ingredients of a life. It was good to see men raised in all kinds of different cultures and backgrounds stand out in these qualities. It was also amazing what could be made out of materials seemingly unfit for any purpose. Coping methods were used to make the best out of a bad situation. I was glad in all of this that: "The Lord is my Shepherd, I shall not want."

Japanese Guardhouse

CHAPTER VI

SHIP RIDE TO JAPAN

ROMANS 8:39, *"Neither height, nor depth, nor any other creature, shall separate us from the love of God, which is in Christ Jesus our Lord."*

Cabanatuan was the headquarters for the P.O.W.s since most details originated or returned there after finishing their project. We were considered expendable so there was always reports about the treatment on the various details. A number of them were extremely harsh and cruel which cost many lives. I especially dreaded the day I would be sent out on an airfield detail. Many beatings were given for not accomplishing the amount of work the Japanese commanders considered necessary.

Then, there were the rumors about work details being sent to Japan or Manchuria. Stories were circulated that some of these details were being used for experimental research. (This was later proven to be true.) American subs on patrol in the China Sea were said to sometimes unknowingly attack ships with American POWs being transported to Japan. The China Sea was known for its rough waters and none of us wanted to be a passenger on an enemy ship with an American torpedo headed our direction. We also realized that our blood was thin due to the heat of the tropics and we did not look forward to a winter in the northern climate of either Manchuria or Japan.

An announcement of a detail headed for Japan was made in September 1943. Cecil and his uncle decided to volunteer for this detail. They contended that this would be a safer time to go to Japan rather than to wait for a later detail. This thinking proved to be logical and accurate, but I wanted to be rescued in the Philippines. It was not my habit to volunteer for anything and I was not about to go on this detail if it was headed for Japan. God wanted me to go and He found the way. The volunteers were far less than the number needed and my name was chosen. Our friend since Fort Bliss, Bill Moore stayed behind at Cabanatuan.

We left another important part of our military in the Philippines, the Chaplains. Many Chaplains were instruments in the hands of God to help many men to accept the Lord Jesus

Christ as their personal Savior. Many men were open to the Biblical plan of salvation by faith in Christ's death, burial and resurrection. Chaplain Taylor, who after the war became Chief of Chaplains, was assigned to the hospital area and did an excellent ministry among the men shortly before they went into eternity. The Chaplaincy included both ministers from the conservative persuasion to the liberal and they did their best to try to help the men in the various camps. The Japanese did not allow any Chaplains to go on the details to Japan. One of the reasons this detail was thought headed for Japan was because no Chaplain had been chosen for it.

Several Chaplains at Cabanatuan knew I planned to go into the ministry after the war. A few days before we left the Philippines, I was called into the Chaplains headquarters and was asked if I would be willing to be the Acting Chaplain of the detail. I was very happy for the opportunity and the arrangement was explained to the American officer in charge of the detail. The Chaplains gave me a regular service song book and three paperbound song booklets. The Japanese had censored only one song, "The Battle Hymn of the Republic". I knew most of the time the chapel services in Japan would have to be conducted on the Q.T.

The day arrived to leave Cabanatuan and we headed for Manila. It was not as crowded on this train trip and when we arrived in Manila, we went immediately to the docks. Port Area was a familiar place and we knew at least part of the trip would be by ship. Perhaps the rumor about going to Japan would prove correct but the ship in the harbor looked too small to take eight hundred fifty of us on our journey. The Japanese had crowded us into boxcars twice before for short trips but surely they would not crowd us on this small ship for a long trip. Three hundred and fifty of us were marched up to our quarters in the front hold of the ship. A look toward the back of the ship revealed the other five hundred would be in the back hold of the ship.

These ships from the Philippines to Japan were later known as the "hell ships" because of the awful conditions. Some trips were worse than ours, where some prisoners became cannibalistic because the Japanese locked them into the holds of the ships without food or water. Some tried to survive by drinking human waste matter, as all human dignity and decency seemed to be destroyed by the treatment designed more for animals instead of fellow human beings. Some of the ships were sunk by torpedoes with a great loss of life to the POWs. The Japanese had used these same ships to ship animals south so they were unclean for the POWs.

Our hold was divided into fourteen bays about ten feet by ten feet and the height of between four and five feet. Each bay had an upper and lower section. Twenty-five men were assigned to each bay. There was more head room on the top, so thirteen men were on top and twelve on the bottom. I was in the lower section. When we tried to sleep, we would put our feet on top of the person opposite us for about an hour and then we would change positions. We thought the other person wanted the longer time period with their feet on top, so naturally there were arguments. All our earthly possessions were in a bag kept under our heads. Magnesium ore was carried in the hold of the ship under us. The guards indicated they were unhappy with us and would gladly shoot us if they could find any kind of an excuse. The topside of the ship contained some open stalls which were our toilets and another area was used for the kitchen area where rice could be boiled. These were blown away in a storm a few days after we left the Philippines. After that we used the open "honey buckets" with no stalls to give any kind of protection or privacy. Honey buckets is a term for buckets used to collect and carry human waste matter. In Japan, the contents are used to fertilize the fields.

Most of the hold was covered with a tarp. There was a ladder to let us climb to topside, but the guards only allowed a few out at a time. A small hole around the ladder was the only open place for fresh air. The hold was very hot and stuffy because of the hot weather and the body heat generated by many men confined to a small area. Periodically, the Japanese would "close down the hatches" and this covered the small opening. This was supposed to happen every night but later the orders were changed and we were happy to have even the small amount of air coming through to us. The hatches were closed during bad weather, or during a sub scare, which happened several times. The heat was unbearable during these times. We tried to spend as much time as possible on topside in order to get some relief from the reality of the ever-present heat, stench and bickering.

Our food and water ration was let down by ropes through the opening. It was times like this that it was necessary to have several friends because if someone was fortunate enough to receive a ration, it could be shared. We guarded our canteens with our lives, because many times it meant the difference between life and death. The three of us slept next to the hull of the ship and kept the canteens in the middle to protect them from thieves. Water was scarce so we would only take a sip and rinse out the entire mouth before swallowing it. The food passed to us in buckets was divided up among the men but it was not always given out in equal portions. Those nearest the food or water received greater portions, and some further away received practically nothing. We were about half-way, so probably received about our share of the precious necessities.

When the ship cleared Manila Bay, it turned north and we were sure our journey would take us from the tropics to a colder climate. Our hold was like a steam bath and we only hoped it would soon get cooler. Some men started talking about the banquets they would have when they returned to the States. Most of us had figured out a two week schedule of banquets in our heads or on a piece of scratch paper. Someone would start to tell their menu and others would join in with theirs. Others would yell for the entire group to shut up because they would rather have a spoonful of rice now instead of the thoughts of the fanciest meal in a few years. The human mind is strange. When the body was starving our thoughts turned to the greatest feast in our imagination. When a minute piece of meat occasionally showed up in our food, we could imagine it as a giant T-bone steak. Even now, I will find myself saving a piece of meat for my last bite. It was our way of coping with the problem and to keep our sanity.

It was fairly dark in the hold of the ship but I was able to read my New Testament. I was glad to study a portion of the Scriptures each day. It was an absolute necessity to have someone in the bay to protect the property of the bay-members. Stealing was the constant threat and New Testaments were a prize steal. Sad to say it was not to read them but it was good paper for the smokers who rolled their cigarettes from salvaged tobacco. Many New Testaments literally went up in smoke. I carried my New Testament everywhere I went so there would be no possibility of losing it.

One day we heard an airplane and from the hum of the motor, we knew it was Japanese. It apparently came out to check on the convoy of ships and we figured we would be in a port within a couple of days. We had a medical corpsman, who had taken ill with appendicitis a couple of days out of Manila. Dr. Keagy did what he could to ease the pain. Dr. Keagy had asked the Japanese to take him off at the next port for the needed surgery. A couple of days later we sailed into the very beautiful harbor at Taipei, Furmosa (Taiwan). Dr. Keagy went to the Japanese with his request and waited for their answer. The Japanese told Dr. Keagy that he would have to operate on board the ship. They did bring him two cans of ether which was enough to keep Joe unconscious during the operation. Dr. Keagy had carried some razor blades and thread since the surrender a year and a half earlier. He came around to the men and asked for the use of some spoons and he bent the handles in a horseshoe shape so as to keep the incision open. The pot of water that was to be made into our evening soup became the vat to sterilize the instruments for surgery. The hold became center stage for what I consider one of the greatest operations. We watched from our bays as the surgery was performed. The incision was made by the razor blade to remove the appendix and Dr. Keagy used the needle and thread he had carried into captivity for his needlework to close the cut. Joe lived and was a valuable asset to our group in Niigata because we did not have a doctor and several of the medical corpsmen served as our medical staff. The Japanese took Dr. Keagy away from us and sent him to Tokyo. He did come to Niigata for a couple of days later on, but that is another story.

The small rations of food and water continued from Furmosa to Japan's mainland. The cooler weather did keep the hold of the ship cooler, which gave some relief. I was one of the few who did not become seasick but I would have if I had stayed in the stench. Whenever possible I tried to get outside. When we went through the edge of a typhoon most of the men were seasick and had no desire to go topside. During the storm I looked out of the small opening and when the ship rolled from side to side, I could see the ocean on that side but it was worse when the ship went into a trough and I was able to see the ocean in front of the ship. The upper structure of the ship kept me from seeing the ocean behind us. Shortly after we came through the storm, we saw land in the distance and were told it was the land of China.

The most eerie part of the trip was the guards with loaded rifles and a machine gun in the ready position. We knew if anything happened to the ship we would be shot. This happened on some of the later ships that were attacked by American subs. The Japanese guards would take out the ladder and fire their machine guns at the helpless prisoners in the hold. There were no markings on the ship to show it was carrying POWs and we were in a convoy of other ships so American ships were unaware of POWs being transported.

We arrived safely in the beautiful harbor of Moji City, Japan. The trip was over and we had made it without meeting a torpedo, hitting a mine, having an air attack or being torn apart in a storm. We were glad the guards did not shoot us on the ship. I took one last look at a guard who looked like one of the characters in "Terry and the Pirates", — only in real life he looked meaner.

It was good to be on solid ground again. Our lungs could be filled with fresh air and the foul smells of the hold were gone. We were taken to the railroad tracks and loaded into passenger cars. It was a relief from the little narrow gauge boxcars of the Philippines. We went through a tunnel to Honshu, the main island of Japan. We travelled through the beautiful country side of southern Honshu. We arrived in Osaka on the following morning, where we transferred to another train. There was a large commotion in the station after disembarking from our train. Everyone started to face toward the north, or away from the ocean and the guards were insistent that we face the same direction. Later, we heard a relative of the Emperor was in a ship sailing past Osaka. The Emperor was thought to be the direct descendent of the sun-god and because this man was a relative, no one was to look in his direction.

The Japanese passed out small boxes of rice, a little seasoned seaweed and a pair of chopsticks along with drinking water. We continued across the mountains to the western coast and up the western coast of Japan to Niigata where we would spend the next twenty-three months.

We had time to think about our future. What would we face in this land of the rising sun? What would be our treatment? What would we eat and where would we work? Gone were the hopes of liberation in the near future because we were too far away from the American supply lines and would have to wait for them to regain island after island. Now, liberation would come only with the invasion of Japan by the United States. We wondered if our motto would become truth:

"Golden gate in Forty-eight,
    I may be late but I can wait."

The country looked untouched by war. Two years later when I rode the train to Tokyo, it would be a different land, a different people and a different story. Tokyo and much of southern Japan would be burned out.

Niigata, 1943
(Photo by the Japanese)

Casper, 1987
(Photo by my son, Len)

85

CHAPTER VII

NIIGATA, JAPAN

I PETER 5:6-7, *"Humble ourselves therefore under the mighty hand of God, that He may exalt you in due time: Casting all your care upon Him: for He careth for you."*

We arrived in the port city of Niigata which is on the western coast of Japan across from Sado Island. It is a little over a hundred miles north of Tokyo but across the mountains on the northwestern coast of Honshu. At the end of the war it was Japan's only open port.

Our group of three hundred fifty were put in a camp with three hundred men captured at Hong Kong. Most of these were Canadians, a few from England and the rest from Holland. We were assigned a space on grass mats of about twenty inches wide by six and a half feet long. The aisles in the building were practically non-existent. Needless to say, being over six feet in height, it left little room for my field bag with my few precious possessions: a mess kit, canteen, and a few items that I had collected over the past eighteen months.

A couple days later our American officers, who had been detained for instructions, arrived at the camp. The Hong Kong prisoners had already been assigned their groups and we were also divided into three working groups. Sietetzu was the group at the foundry, Rinko worked at the coal yards and my group, called Marutzu, worked on the docks as stevedores.

It was the middle of October and the weather seemed very cold because we had come from the tropics. We had to stay close together because of the space allotment and also to keep warm. The Japanese issued us five very thin blankets which were about as warm as two G.I. blankets. The Japanese issued us some heavier clothing which they had taken away from the Canadians. The windows of the barracks had sliding wooden panels to cover them at night which helped to keep heat inside the buildings.

The fall rains caused us to be cold and miserable in the forty degree temperatures. We were given straw raincoats on the job, but they failed to repel the water after a couple hours. We returned to camp cold and wet and slept on our clothes so they would be a little drier by the next morning -- but they would still be damp.

Our water supply was pumped from a contaminated shallow well. After learning it was unsafe to drink (the hard way), we drank only the water at the docks and carried a canteen of water into camp.

My last memory of this camp was having to witness the torture of a fellow prisoner who broke some minor rule. He was tied to a post at the gate of the camp. We marched past him twice every day and listened to his cries during the night. We watched him die as an example to the rest of us. The temperatures were below freezing and it took almost five days for him to die from exposure and gangrene. The Sietetzu group remained behind as the Rinko and Marutzu groups left for their new barracks. There were four dormitories which would hold one hundred men each at the new camp. Our living quarters were without heat.

We heard about the communal bath houses in Japan. The first couple of baths at Niigata were in a communal bath house. The prisoners of war were supposed to have the bath house to themselves, but there was a steady flow of traffic through the bath house. The gender of our visitors was not given any consideration. Later a bath house was built at the prison camp and we were able to take our baths in private. A large tank was built which was probably about twenty by sixty feet in size. It was about four feet in height with the water level at three feet. The water was kept at about 120 degrees or as hot as possible without burning us. We were required to soap and rinse off before entering the tank. The hot water nearly took our breath away and it would turn us a bright pink. Nevertheless, we looked forward to bath day.

We were beginning to get acquainted with our work and what was expected of us on the job. Most of the townspeople ignored us, but there were some who expressed their hatred for us by their attitude. We did not know the language, but it was easy to understand their actions. Some children would spit at us, or throw rocks, and call us names.

I had a life-long habit of measuring everything; so I did my usual thing and stepped off the size of the camp, and each building. I also counted the number of steps from camp to the docks and the size of each building on the docks. This may seem a foolish thing to do,—after all who would ever use it— but it was a way to retain my thinking ability. It gave my mind something to do while going through the motions of forced labor.

The New Year's Eve which ushered in the year of 1944 is one I shall always remember. Many believers plan a Watchnight service so as to bring in the New Year with prayer. 1944 came in with a bang for me, because my barracks collapsed. Several men were killed or injured but I was asleep in the upper bunk and did not awaken until someone lifted a beam that pinched my head. The Japanese had taken our pictures and stored them in the office of the barracks where I had been sleeping. When the prisoners found them during the clean-up, they gave them to the men, who hid them individually until we were liberated. I was one who had my picture and returned to the States with it.

The Japanese moved us to another barracks in the compound. The barracks were about twenty-eight feet wide and seventy-five to eighty feet long. The structure was a double decker and built to house one hundred men. It had a dirt floor with an aisle through the middle. There was a step of about one foot from the aisle into our sleeping bays which were about nine and a half feet long.

The lower part of the bay had a foot and a half wide section next to the outside wall made of a wooden board. This left an eight foot wide grass mat next to the aisle. Several of us on the bottom bays cut out a section of the wooden board and used it to hide our contraband. Occasionally the Japanese would search the barracks but our secret hiding place was never found. Several times I was caught on my days off with contraband out, but the guards were usually looking for specific things. Contraband would include a variety of things: such as paper, maps from Japanese newspapers, and anything questionable brought in from work details. Once a guard came over to look at something I had which was "illegal". We talked about it, but as soon as he left I hid it. About twenty minutes later, he must have remembered he saw something illegal, and he returned to our barracks. The ten or twelve men in the barracks suddenly could not understand what he was hunting for or what he was saying.

The Japanese finally put in a half of a 55 gallon drum for a stove and we were able to have a couple hours of fire in the evenings. This allowed us to warm up from the cold after a hard day of work. The Japanese gave us ten sen (five cents) a day for our work. It was enough to provide a little package of tea each month and we could make tea on top of the stove in our canteens. Some smokers purchased "hair tobacco". It looked like ground up stems of tobacco plants and it was smoked in a small pipe. We cooked contraband food inside the stove but were never caught. The guards would come into the barracks with the smell of cooking food. They would grab the canteens off the stove and empty them; then they would shake their heads when the canteens only contained water. We were very glad we were never caught with the "quan", a name given to any food being cooked.

Food was our main concern. We knew the ration we received was barely sufficient to keep body and soul together. The food ration was better in Japan, but the expended energy while doing heavier work in colder weather burned more calories. On the first Christmas eve in Japan, the camp commander told us that he realized the next day was a very special holiday, therefore he would honor it by giving us the day off from work, and would only cut our rations in half. We received very few Red Cross packages during our internment. The men held in Tokyo said there were warehouses in that area which were full of packages, but we would receive a package to divide between two men about three times a year.

One day after packages had come into camp one of the POWs saw a guard washing his clothes and complained about the poor American soap. The prisoner asked him if he would trade it for a piece of Japanese soap, which he was glad to do. After the trade, the American cut off the outside edges of his purchase and enjoyed the cheese.

We liked to have something a little extra on special days. The highlight of my extra food in Japan was on our second Christmas. Bates had made a canteen into a dutch oven. One day he worked on butter at the docks and was able to salvage about a quarter of a pound. We each brought an apple into camp that week. One day I was able to get some flour, and Bates managed to bring some sugar and cinnamon for our quan. We cooked it on the inside of the stove. We were worried when a guard came into the barracks because that pie was giving off an excellent aroma. Our canteens on top of the stove were emptied but our pie was cooked to perfection. We thought of the Scripture verse, "Thou preparest a table before me in the presence of mine enemies:"

Our first winter in Japan was extremely snowy with about twenty-five to thirty feet of snow. The road to work consisted of about eight feet of packed snow. The houses and small stores along the way had tunnels into them. My feet were frost-bitten the second winter in Japan which caused my big toe-nails to turn black every year for ten years after returning to the States. Quite a few men died because of the cold weather.

The Sietetzu group worked inside the foundry on many dangerous jobs. The Rinko group worked on coal that came on ships from Manchuria. Some of the men worked in the hold of the ships loading nets which would be dumped onto a barge. Then, it went by conveyer belts into small coal cars. Prisoners had to push these cars along the trestle, and dumped them into large railroad cars. Often men would fall about twenty feet from the tracks to the ground and would hurt their hands and feet. Sometimes railroad cars were loaded from a nearby pile of coal. Four men worked together on this detail; two had shovels and two carried yea-hoe baskets. After the baskets were loaded, the men walked a small plank to dump the baskets of coal into the rail car. If the yea-hoe baskets were not correctly balanced, they would swing and make a person fall. Some men were dumped into the bay because they were unable to balance the baskets. Sometimes the POWs were able to load rocks into the coal cars.

Our stevedore's work at Marutzu for the first year was mostly to load pig-iron. The Japanese chose two leaders from among the fifty American prisoners. These two leaders each had about a dozen men who went with them all the time. The rest of us were split up into one of the groups that worked on pig-iron. We had to average fifteen tons of pig-iron per man per day. We must throw it from the ground into railroad cars. Boxcars were harder to fill than the flat cars because we would have to load the center first, then fill the ends from the center. After that, we had to fill up the center again. Naturally, all three groups (foundry, coal yard, and docks) thought they had the worst detail. Our detail on the docks did end up being the best detail, but at first, I still think it was the worst.

We filled a car with pig-iron, then pushed it down the tracks and brought back empties. During the night a switch engine took the full cars and would leave more empties for us to fill the next day. Many days in the winter we would have to dig the pig-iron out of the snow and ice. Our hands would be so cold and raw that we would lose feeling in them. One day, I hit my hand on the edge of the boxcar and my hand stung for a few minutes. I worked the rest of the morning and went into the mess hall at noon. My hand began to sting when the warmth of the room brought feeling back into my hand. I found that my fingers were badly bruised and a couple of my fingers nails were black and one almost torn off.

Fifty of the Hong Kong group who worked on an adjoining pier lived in the same barracks with us. We were on the north side of the building, and they were on the south. Several of their group were from the States but had gone to Canada to sign up for the war. They had a tragedy shortly before the end of the war. A group of them were working in a warehouse when one man thought he found some alcohol and about a half dozen men drank it. It was anti-freeze for the high flying airplanes. They became ill about dinner time and died in agony about midnight. One man did survive because he drank so much he vomited.

Several coolies (lowest working class) who worked on the docks near us had ox-carts. They would load their carts as the ships unloaded the nets of pig-iron onto the docks. They would bring their ox-carts into the area that we had cleared out, and unload them onto the ground. We asked them to bring the carts to the boxcars and let us unload them but they refused. It would be easier for us to load the railroad cars from the carts. We could get our quota easier and they would earn more money because they were paid by the number of cart loads they delivered.

One day a coolie lady drove her cart close to us. One of the men grabbed the ox and took the cart up to the railroad car. A couple of us got on each end of the cart and unloaded it into the boxcar. The coolie lady was happy with the arrangement and would bring her cart to us whenever possible. When the men coolies realized that she made many more trips, they let us unload their carts also. The carts were probably thirty to thirty-six inches high and the boxcars were about four feet high. It is a lot easier to throw pig-iron fifteen inches instead of four feet. We proved the adage that "laziness is the mother of invention".

In the late spring of 1944, one of the groups worked on something other than pig-iron. Later, both groups worked on other things being loaded into the warehouses. The last year in Japan we worked on just about everything that passed into or out of the docks: all kinds of grain, fruit, vegetables, fish, beancakes, baggage, seaweed, heavy freight, military goods, a money shipment, canned goods, and the always present pig-iron. Two ships made regular trips from Korea with soy beans which were so necessary to the diet of the Japanese. The bags of beans were ninety kilo (198 pounds) and we carried them all day. We would either stack them in warehouses or carry them into boxcars.

We ate raw beans whenever possible and would occasionally manage to smuggle a few back into camp. This would end up as a contest with the guards to see if we could take some food into camp. When we lost, it meant a beating by the guard. One day one of our foremen had a man take part of a sack of soy beans to our mess-shack and the next day we were given a cup of bean soup. This became a daily habit and that extra cup of soup certainly helped our health. We had two Japanese foremen, Pop and the Old Man, for the two years in Japan. They were good to us and at times would look the other way when we took food. They were required to work us hard every day, but they tried to be fair with us.

It was during the last ten months that one of the guards suggested that we should have some parched beans at the end of the day. At first it was only once in a while but they must have seen an improvement in our health and ability to work so they later made it a daily practice. No doubt this was a factor in helping some of the Marutzu group survive. This is why I said our detail was the best at the end of the war, but I considered our provisions came from the Lord.

One of the first details other than pig-iron, occurred during fishing season. Ship loads of fish were brought in and we had to unload them. The guards were unable to watch very closely when we threw the boxes of fish from one to another. We soon learned to feel the fish to see if it had eggs or sperm. If we found eggs, we could strip the eggs with one swipe of a finger and bring the eggs to our mouth as we reached for the next box. Sometimes during a short break we would flay a fish, put it in the sun and if we had a chance we would eat it on our way back to the mess shack. The bad part was that the fishing season only lasted from ten days to two weeks. Many fish were infested with hook worms and it was amazing that all of us didn't end up with hook worms. If we were working on anything edible, we looked for opportunities to sample it, even though most of it would never pass the Department of Agriculture test for pure food.

We were envious of the "cliques" who controlled the work assignments and food. American leaders were chosen because of their numbers. We had the prison numbers of 301 through

350 in our Marutzu group. The Japanese picked 301 and 302 for group leaders. My POW number in Japan was 331.

Usually our American leader and his buddies worked inside the box cars and the rest of us carried the bags or boxes. They were protected from the eyes of the guards. When they disappeared inside the car for a few minutes, we knew they were enjoying the samples of food, but occasionally the rest of us would have the opportunity to get some of the goodies. One day some of the men worked on a butter shipment. The Japanese must not have known much about butter because when a can broke open the Americans were allowed to wipe it on their shoes, but if they tried to taste it, they were slapped. They were told it would make them ill, but a friend of mine smuggled about a quarter pound into camp, where it was put to good use.

We saw large disks of bean cakes that were two feet in diameter. We started to eat some of it but our Japanese foreman told us it was made from the sweepings off the docks and pressed together to make animal feed. We lost our taste for it, but sometimes it was a temptation when the rations were short. The extra soup and parched beans practically ended eating bean cake.

I was in very poor health when we arrived in Japan and not well during most of the time, even though I gained some strength during the last few months. Two men were assigned to carry the water bucket each day and I was usually given this duty. We would go over to the Japanese kitchen, while the others marched to the docks. Our mess shack, the Japanese kitchen and the headquarters were near the entrance to the dock area. We would take our water bucket to the faucet at the back of the kitchen. The Japanese cooks must have felt sorry for us. They would yell at us, but they usually had a few crusts of bread and some cooked fish heads to give us. The scraps were laid on the edge of a concrete wall and we enjoyed the little extra food. A fish-brain sandwich may not sound appetizing, but it helped fill a vacuum. This is why I was willing to carry the water bucket.

One guard sometimes gave me the job of counting the number of bags or pieces of freight loaded into box cars. This was an easy job which helped me survive. I reached the place where I could think my numbers in Japanese. If someone showed me a number and asked me what it was, I would have probably answered them in Japanese.

Sometimes we worked at the Fish House where fish items were kept frozen. We worked there about a half dozen times and enjoyed the frozen fish, especially the raw squid. We had to eat it frozen and raw; even though it may not have been the best way to eat it, because frozen fish has little taste. We were not watched very closely at the Fish House, so we took advantage of the opportunity. Some of the men of Rinko thought all of us at Marutzu had opportunities for extra food every day, but most of us seldom brought extra food into camp.

Occasionally, we worked on fruit or vegetables and usually we could eat a few raw vegetables or fruit. If we took an orange, it meant we must eat the peal so there would be no evidence of the departed orange. The guards tried to keep us from taking anything. If a guard was coming close, we would yell, "Air raid" to warn all the POWs that they better be careful. A few times a guard would slip up on someone with contraband but another man would "accidentally" bump the guard and knock him off balance long enough for the guilty man to be able to get rid of the "salvos". (If you were caught it was stealing; but if not caught, it was called salvos)

Freight was interesting because of the variety. One of our Japanese foremen would occasionally show us how much he could carry. Once I saw him carry a box of around 300 kilo (660 pounds). We would brag on him and not outdo him or reveal how much we could carry so he would not expect us to carry larger loads. Toward the end of the war when my strength improved, I was able to carry two bags of beans or about 400 pounds, but would not do it when the Japanese were around our group.

The Japanese attitude toward women was strange to us. The women of America should be thankful to live in our culture instead of theirs. It is only where the Judeo-Christian values have gone that women are respected instead of being considered a slave. Love seemed unknown in Japan. One day I was told to report to some coolies working on a bean carrying detail. The coolie foreman asked me if I had my hooks and I told him that I did. He told me to get up into the boxcar and stack. I asked him to repeat the orders because I thought I had misunderstood him, but he repeated the same command. Here I, a prisoner-of-war whom they considered very low class was ordering the coolie women where to drop the bags of beans. All I had to do was to put the last few bags into place and close the boxcar.

One day we worked on a cargo that we knew was carrots

because of the smell. A friend took the end of a carrot and at the same time he dropped the bag. This allowed the carrot to come out in his hand and he planned on eating it later. We were surprised to see a three foot carrot in his hand. It was impossible to hide in the palm of his hand so he was caught stealing the vegetable. A guard was standing near where we were unloading and he hit my friend with a crow bar. My friend broke his nose on the concrete surface and when he regained consciousness, he was told to go back to work without any inspection of his wounds. He had a terrible headache for the rest of the day and night.

Only a few Japanese could drive a car and they would look at us with disbelief when we said we could all drive a vehicle. One guard brought up the subject of driving cars and told us he did not believe we could all drive. He took us over to a truck and lined up our detail of twenty-four men. Each one of us had to back the truck about twenty feet and then drive it forward to park it. He was surprised when all drove the truck and shook his head in disbelief. He threw his stick to the ground instead of using it on one of us. Guards carried a stick about the length of a baseball bat and several inches in diameter. These were used to beat us when they thought we were not working hard enough, or did something they did not like, or sometimes, just for no reason at all. We nicknamed these sticks, "vitamin sticks".

We studied our guards to figure out how they would react under certain situation. We watched how close each one would watch us and how strict would be their reaction. We were at the disadvantage, so we had to manipulate our situation. Sometimes if their attention could be diverted, other POWs could accomplish their goal of obtaining something considered illegal.

Japanese varied as much as any other nationality. Some guards treated us fairly well, while others were looking for something to blame on us, or beat us for the smallest offenses. A couple of guards were a little less than six feet but considered themselves tall and would beat any POW taller than themselves. Those of us who were tall tried to stay away from them and we appreciated the cooperation the shorter prisoners gave us when they allowed us to load or unload away from the sight of the guards. I was beaten on several occasions by these guards.

Several guards who were decent to us would suddenly turn

on us for no reason. Once a prisoner pushed a guard out of the way of a train and saved his life, but within a half hour this guard turned on his rescuer and gave him a brutal beating. We were working on a salmon boat and the guard took a smoked salmon and literally wore it out on my face. After I returned home, my dentist told me that the roots of my two front teeth had died and were probably caused by a beating I had received or a hard blow to the chin. It was probably at this occasion my teeth received the damage.

We had several different types of guards. The first group was our camp guards who took us to and from work. They were attached to the military and were changed every couple of months. They did not stay at the docks during the day, but would return for us at the end of our working hours. Several civilian guards remained at the dock area while we worked. They were supposed to guard us but they knew we would not escape so they did not watch us all the time.

Two Japanese foremen supervised our work and gave permission to go to the bathroom or leave the work detail. Sometimes our foremen could loan us to a coolie foreman who needed men for a few hours. Each warehouse had a foreman who watched us work at his warehouse. The dock guards were civilians from Niigata and were usually better to us than the camp guards.

One day the head foreman asked our group foreman what the Americans were working on for that day. Our foreman said, "Pig-iron" and it was funny to watch them as their voices increased in volume as the question was repeated and the same answer given. Our foreman finally realized he was using an English word while talking to his Japanese foreman.

We always tried to find something amusing so we could stand the pressures of prison life. We had to stand at rigid attention every morning and evening for roll call which lasted about fifteen minutes. During the winter the evening roll-call was in the aisle of the barracks. Our barracks was the first inspected so after the Japanese officer passed, the men on the back row sat on the edge of the bays.

One evening a guard looked in a window and saw Ernie sitting down on the bay. He rushed into the barracks and decided to make an example out of Ernie's poor behavior. The guard thought a bawling out by Hank, our group leader, would be better punishment than a slapping. Hank stood in front of

Ernie as commanded and with the meanest frown and the harshest voice, he pointed his finger into Ernie's face and yelled, "Ernie, as far as I am concerned you can sit down anytime possible". Ernie laughed out loud and the rest of us snickered. The guard looked at the angry frown, listened to Ernie's laughter, and snickering prisoners and could not understand what was happening. The confused body language caused the guard to turn and run out of the barracks at top speed. We did not have any more problem with that guard. I wish all of our guard problems could have been resolved this easily. One day I was working on the docks and had a load of vegetables on my shoulder when I saw a guard swing at my mid section with a long hook. I rolled with the punch but my shirt was torn and my flesh had a long scratch. If I had not seen the start of his swing, I would have been opened up just above the naval. I never did know the reason for the attack but I was thankful the Lord helped me to see the hook in time to get out of the way of the full force of the blow.

Language is always a barrier between people of different cultures and was constantly causing problems in our dealings with the Japanese. Many times we would depend on the facial expressions or actions to understand what was wanted. There were times when we did not want to understand, and we would shrug our shoulders and say in Japanese, "I don't understand". This sometimes would relieve the pressure and keep us from being punished. We spoke a Japanese-English mixed language at Marutzu.

It is hard for civilized people to realize the extreme sadistic nature of the Japanese. Cruelty was first nature to them and torture was their chief weapon of ruling their own people. Americans cannot fully understand the Japanese because their customs are altogether different from ours. Under their caste system, the children would follow the vocation of their father. Anyone of a higher caste could, without the least provocation, command a subordinate to stand at attention and be slapped or struck without recourse. These brutal customs tend to make sadists of those reared in this atmosphere.

One of our guards had been a prisoner of the Chinese. We felt compassion for this guard because the Chinese had amputated a joint a day until he lost about half of his toes and fingers. He realized there would soon be too many joints missing for him to live so he decided to escape from his captors. He made it back to the Japanese lines and they sent him back to Japan to guard us. He was one of the best guards we had all of the time we were prisoners. After the Americans had dropped the atom bomb and the surrender was being negotiated, he came to the American prisoners of war and asked if any of us had anything against him. If we did then he would allow us to punish him. He was told that no one held anything against him.

The nadir of my torture took place in January, 1944 when infection developed in my right ankle. I took my shoe off at noon but the swelling continued, so a dock guard told me to clean up a shed in the afternoon. The camp guard came into the mess shack and asked me why my shoe was not on my foot. I showed him that it was so swollen that I could not put it on. He picked up my shoe and struck my sore ankle with it many times. I could scarcely keep from crying as the pain was so excruciating. After seeing the pain on my face, he repeated the blows just for the pleasure of inflicting pain. He would give a silly laugh after each blow on the ankle. I had to be carried to camp that evening and was taken to the so-called hospital.

The Lord again worked in marvelous ways in my behalf. Major Keagy, the doctor who had performed the great surgery in the hold of the ship, was sent to Niigata for two days. He checked into the other camp and was not needed there. He came to our camp the next day and still had no patients who needed surgery. This was the day I was carried into camp. Cecil brought Dr. Keagy over to the hospital and showed him my foot. He put me on a table and told Cecil to stand at my head. He told me to grab the legs of the table because he was going to operate on a cellutitis and bone infection. He had no anesthetic, so he said, "Preacher, grit your teeth". He made an incision on each side of my ankle and then took a steel wire to scrape the bone. There was over a canteen cup of puss drained out of the ankle.

He put some type of dressing in the incision and told me to take it out in a few days. The ankle began to heal and I went back to work in about a month. An English doctor came to camp and he was surprised that I was able to stand on the ankle, let alone work on it every day. The Lord was my Great Physician.

On Christmas of 1944 I became ill with pneumonia and laid in the barracks for about a week before I was moved to the hospital. There was a stove in the building but no fuel. Cecil would conceal coal in his clothes and bring it to the hospital to make a small fire to keep me warm. Wendell worked on the docks and he borrowed fruit from boxes which he brought over to me. The Lord used both of these men to help me recover.

A couple of months before our liberation I had a dry fish bone enter the middle finger of my right hand. The Doctor put ichthyoul ointment on it but it kept getting worse. I figured it needed to be operated on but the doctor refused to do it. I put my trusty razor blade in boiling water to sterilize it. I placed my finger on a box where I kept a few personal belongings. I cut out the fish bone with my left hand. Even though it bled a great deal I was able to remove all of the fish bone. The doctor told me I was very stupid to operate on myself but another man followed the doctor's orders and had to have his finger amputated after we were liberated. The Canadian man later had to have his arm amputated because of the infection caused by a fish bone. Although it looked like I had done a stupid act while in prison, I am sure the Lord was my Helper in that time of need.

All of us suffered from malnutrition throughout the entire time as prisoners. The food was a little better in Japan but we lacked many of the needed vitamins. The men working on the docks were able to get some extra food, but most of it was eaten raw and infested with germs. Our food had little if any salt in it but occasionally we could get a little salt to add to our diet. I would not put it in the food because when I ran out of salt it was hard to return to food without seasoning. I would put my salt into my tea because I could drink the tea with or without salt.

I have already told about the different food we ate in the Philippines. While in Japan hunger drove us to eat: seal meat, snails, octopus (all of these raw), cat, dog, and grasshoppers that had been prepared in soy sauce. I was offered roasted rat a couple of times but declined. Our soup was usually made out of wide thick seaweed, the tops of vegetables, and occasionally dried fish. The ration of grain was usually maize or barley. The maize looked like red buck-shot and tasted like it. We did not get very much rice because it was needed for the Japanese. We were given about two-thirds of a pound per day but the ration did increase the last few months as the American forces drew nearer to Japan. I still like to eat rice but I have refused to eat barley in any form.

One guard took a liking to me and would occasionally give me a little extra food. One evening as we started for camp he slipped me about a pound bag of parched beans. I had them under a cartridge belt but our camp guard decided to search us. He found the "illegal" bag of beans, threw them on the ground and slapped me a few times. Something happened and he was called away for a few minutes. The dock guard slipped the beans back to me. The camp guard searched me four times and each time he found the beans, he slapped me but the dock guard would give me the beans. On the way back to camp, the camp guard walked up and down the lines looking for me. He could not find me because I had traded places to an inside column. I was able to get the beans to camp and my friends and I really enjoyed those beans. After those four beatings I was certainly glad I was not caught the fifth time.

On Good Friday of 1945, a guard who liked us took about ten of us to a barge to work on apples. On the way to the barge, he told us we would be by ourselves and we could eat some apples. We really took advantage of the golden opportunity and ate until we were filled up. We had been working on pig-iron all month without a break and one man on the apple detail had vowed that he would not eat extra food on Good Friday. After working about two hours we saw him eating an apple and reminded him about his vow. He told us that he remembered we were a day ahead of American time and Good Friday would be the next day in the States. The next day we were back on pig-iron and he kept his vow. Pig-iron is not good eating — definitely, not good pork.

At first the Japanese made us work three weeks without a day off and then they started to give us one day off in ten. Finally, they decided to give everyone the first Sunday and third Saturday of each month. We also got one more day off but this depended on the last number of our prison number. Since my number was 331, I received the eleventh or twenty-first off depending on the month. This system gave me twice a month that I could have services for all the men who desired to attend. It was not easy to have a church service because we had to have it on the Q.T. (quiet). Usually, I put a note on the bulletin board that I was holding services at my bunk or at the hospital. The Japanese stayed out of the hospital, so it was fairly safe to conduct services there. Every week I would try to have a Bible study or message. When someone passed away, I could have a special service for them.

I did not learn enough Japanese to converse with the coolies about the things of the Bible. Our conversation was a mixture of English, military and coolie Japanese. The last Japanese commander had graduated from the University of California with high honors. After he took command he decided he would allow a Christian funeral service for the first American to die. He asked our highest American officer, Colonel Fellows, to contact the American Chaplain and have him prepare for the funeral service.

All of the higher officials of the companies we worked for were invited to the services and many could understand English. The Japanese Commander told me to give a Christian service and he would conclude with a Japanese service. I used I CORINTHIANS 15:3-4 for the text of the message. My sermon gave the reason for our faith in the Lord Jesus Christ: that Christ died for our sins, was buried and rose again on the third day. This means that we have the only religion whose founder arose triumphant from the tomb and that His people would also rise again from the grave. I had this opportunity to preach the Gospel message of salvation through Christ Jesus. I prayed that in some way some in Niigata would have the opportunity to believe in Jesus Christ as their Savior. The Lord answered my prayers in an unusual way.

Seventeen years after I was liberated from Japan I was visiting a good friend in Cherokee, Iowa. Pastor Bob Lehn told me he would like for me to meet a doctor who had recently moved into the city. The doctor was Japanese. When Bob introduced us he told the doctor that I had been a Japanese prisoner of war. The doctor seemed fearful until my friend told him that I did not hold grudges against my captors. The doctor asked me where I was held and I told him I worked on the docks at Niigata. He asked me if I could remember a group of boys who would throw rocks or spit on us and call us names. He told me that he was one of those boys who lived near the docks and tried to give us trouble. His uncle had a business near the docks.

He later went to the University at Tokyo and won a scholarship to a medical school in Philadelphia. While he was in medical school a Filipino won a scholarship to the same school. This Filipino had accepted Christ as his Savior as a teenager and planned to return to the Philippines to help his people. When he saw the Japanese student, all the anger of the war years returned. He decided he would get revenge for all the atrocities that had been done to him, his family, friends and nation.

One night he was determined to kill the Japanese student

but the Lord kept him from committing murder. A Bible Presbyterian Medical Missionary was also taking advance medical training at the same school. The Filipino student discussed his plan with the missionary who advised him to pray for the conversion of the Japanese doctor. He reminded him of his responsibility of trying to reach the former enemy for Christ. The Filipino went to the Japanese and asked for forgiveness for having hatred in his heart. The Japanese doctor listened to this amazing testimony and not only forgave the Filipino but trusted Christ as his own personal Savior.

He gave this testimony to me and the doctor asked if I could speak Japanese because his wife did not speak English. I admitted that I only spoke coolie and military Japanese but that did not bother the doctor. We went to his home and I met his wife who had just come from Japan. She was delighted to find someone who spoke her language. It was an interesting experience and one which I will always treasure. The doctor prayed that his wife would come to know Christ as her personal Savior. I certainly hope the Lord used this doctor to win others to our Lord when he returned home. I pray that some of those other boys who gave us a hard time at Niigata will come to know our wonderful Savior.

The isolation we suffered caused us to know little about the events of the war years. It seems we are always trying to catch up on the history of those years. We found out how the war was going by looking for Japanese newspapers on the docks. If any of them contained maps, we would ask the Navy chiefs who had been in the Orient for years to tell us where the island was that was shown on the maps. The maps showed that the war was moving back toward the Philippines Islands. When a map showed Luzon, we all knew the battles were getting closer. We could not understand that sometimes the islands were on a line with Guam. Our questions were answered after we learned there were two fronts; one headed through the Philippines and the other east of the Philippines coming up through the small island chains. The maps of Furmosa made us think it would not be long before the invasion of Japan.

The first American airplane to fly over us thrilled our hearts because they were land based planes. One day in April, 1945, we heard the air raid sirens for the first time and an American plane flew over us. The next month there was another plane and on June 20th planes dropped mines into the harbor which they did every four or five nights. One day when we were unloading a bean ship we looked up at the entrance of the harbor when the next bean ship entered the harbor. It hit a mine and was soon sinking. We yelled and shouted for joy but the guards hit and slapped us for our expressions of ecstasy.

The first dive bombing attack at Niigata was on July 17th when the planes came in and bombed the airfield and oil refinery. There were a few machine gun bursts near the docks. We were working at the fish house and took cover by some coal piles at the edge of the docks. One of the American planes crashed near the breakwater of the harbor. The planes were gone before the sirens blew for the city of Niigata. The raid gave us a boost because we knew the Americans were close enough to use dive bombers. The Japanese began to get serious about the war and started to build some bomb shelters on the docks and along the roads.

We were working on the docks on August 10th, when we again heard the short blasts of the sirens to signal the approach of raiding planes. We hastily left the work area and were taken to our shack which was about fifty yards from the edge of the docks. The Japanese had a destroyer about fifty yards from us. The battle raged furiously about us for a few minutes. Again the Lord was with us because not one prisoner was injured. The shack didn't provide much protection but it was better than the old heavy beamed warehouse used in a practice drill. The warehouse was in such weakened condition that I was more concerned about having the heavy beams fall on us than the bombs.

Single planes had been unnoticed but now whenever a single plane flew over there was a lot of excitement among the Japanese. We knew something big had happened to change their attitude toward a single plane and especially the B-29s. On the twelfth of August pamphlets were dropped on Niigata and the entire city was evacuated overnight, with the exception of the Japanese Army and the prisoners of war. The morning of August fifteenth our guards were very excited at the docks. They talked among themselves and paid no attention to us. We tried to follow the conversation and knew something big had taken place which involved the B-29s or at least one B-29.

Our liberation from abuse, filthy living, insufficient medical attention, starvation and isolation was beginning to take place. While our liberation was cause for great rejoicing, it doesn't compare with the great Liberation of mankind when

103

the Lord Jesus Christ arose from the grave after going to the Cross of Calvary for the sins of mankind. We are prisoners of sin by nature and need to be liberated but one must accept God's way of salvation by accepting Jesus Christ as their personal Savior. JOHN 1:12, "But as many as receive Him to them gave He power to become the sons of God even to them that believe on His name."

I have been asked my opinion on the use of the A-bomb. Niigata was a danger spot for the target of the bombs. It was the secondary target for the second bomb and a pilot told us that Niigata was the target for the third bomb if it had been needed. We did not know what he was talking about in the note he dropped to us at camp. Later we found out the words he wrote to us were correct and Niigata would have been a prime target. If the third bomb would have been necessary to end the hostilities, it would have been worth it even if it would have ended my life. The A-bomb in reality saved millions of lives not only American but Japanese if an invasion would have been necessary. Plans were formed that every American prisoner would have been murdered the moment the first Americans landed on Japanese soil. If there had been a choice, instant death by a bomb would have been favored over the slow torture death by the Japanese. It took the words of the Emperor who was considered deity, to bring an end to the fighting by the people.

Niigata Camp (Origin of Picture Unknown)

104

CHAPTER VIII

LIBERATION

GALATIANS 3:20, *"Now unto Him that is able to do exceeding abundantly above all that we ask or think, according to the power that worketh in us."*

JOHN 10:9, *"I am the door: by me if any man enter in, he shall be saved, and shall go in and out and find pasture."*

I had never kept a diary in the United States but thought it would be interesting to record my journey overseas. When we surrendered, I destroyed the entries from the start of the war through the four months of the battle so nothing of importance would be given to the Japanese.

The excited Japanese on the docks pointed to some major changes in the war on the fifteenth of August. At this time I began another diary so I could have a record of the liberation. I recorded the events in the book where I kept a roster of Battery E of the 200th C.A. (A.A.). The events indicated the war would soon end or the Americans would soon make an invasion of Japan.

AUGUST 16 — We were lined up ready to go to work but a guard came out of headquarters and the formation was dismissed. I am determined to keep an accurate record of our liberation or our closing days in case we do not survive. The events of the morning gave me an eerie feeling.

We were called out for a wood-carrying detail in the afternoon. We went to a small grove of trees and carried out some small logs for fires in camp. A couple of guards, including the one who was a Chinese P.W. told us that the war was over. The attitude of the Japanese was one of complete dejection. We waited for tinko (roll call), but no announcement about the war situation.

AUGUST 17 — We started to fall out at the regular time this morning but all details were called off. Something big has happened because the ex-P.W. guard told one of the men that if anyone had anything against him, then he would allow them to beat on him because America had won the war. We were able to rest but our group was called out late in the afternoon to bring chow into camp.

There is no official word about the war but there is movement outside camp, as though the civilians are moving back into Niigata. This fact gives added implication that some negotiations are being made about a treaty. I am surprised because I figured the Japanese war lords would force a fight to the finish.

AUGUST 18 — Yasumi (rest) day brings hopes this will be my last official day as a P.O.W., and I hope to start home by next month. This was my day to carry chow from the kitchen to the barracks. I held church services in the bath house at 1:00 P.M., with a good attendance and the attitude was far better. We are collecting addresses of friends and are looking forward to returning home. There was a music program in the afternoon. We had a special dinner tonight, goat stew and apple sauce with our regular ration of food.

AUGUST 19 — Another day of rest, while we wait for some announcements. The war must be over, but a suspense fills the air. It is good to walk around at night without being under blackout rules.

Cecil and I talked about our plans for the future. I plan to go to Bible College to prepare for the Lord's work. The Lord has had a purpose for these past years and the experience as acting chaplain has helped me relate to the needs of the men. I spent the afternoon drawing to relax. We have received more rice the past few days and some was given away tonight, but we need more vegetables.

AUGUST 20 — A great announcement was made last night by the Japanese office. It was officially announced at tinko that the war has ended, but the terms of the surrender have not been arranged. It seems like we have awakened out of a horrible nightmare or this is a wonderful dream too good to be true. Last night I had a wonderful peaceful rest with the release of the pressure. I spent the morning cleaning up my mess equipment and reading Scripture.

AUGUST 21 — Four years ago today, Cecil and Marthabelle were married. A few days later we left for the Philippines. Cecil is naturally looking forward to seeing her. I have heard Cecil mention her so much that I feel I know her. I found some paper when working at the docks, so I spent several hours drawing in the afternoon. I stepped off the distances of buildings and other landmarks at the docks and I have almost completed my map of the docks. I still have a little to do to complete my map of the road to work. Probably no one will ever use it, but it has helped me.

Our anxiety to leave Niigata has increased. Has time stopped? Departure day can not come too soon. Rumors really flew with the arrival of the Japanese transportation officer. We received a few letters into camp and I heard from Mom and Bertha. Mom has not mentioned anything about Dad, and Bertha has not mentioned Rush. He would probably be in service and she would not mention him because of security reasons. Cecil and I ate dinner together tonight.

AUGUST 22 — A group went swimming this morning but I did not go with them. We organized a softball game in the afternoon outside camp in a level area. Our side won 11 to 2 and I played third base. I had two hits in four at-bats. I imagine we were quite a sight trying to play after four years of no practice.

Rations were raised about a week ago from slightly less than a pound per day and today it was raised to 700 grams per day which is about a pound and a half. I guess they are trying to fatten us before liberation.

Our Japanese Camp Commander called out the group leaders and announced that he was leaving us. We learned more about him and now understand some of the strange things he had done. He graduated from California University as an honor student. We were surprised at his perfect English in his first speech to us when he kicked the interpreter in the seat of the trousers and sent him into the guard house. He spoke in Japanese and then he translated it into English. One night last spring while he was drinking, he had the four piece band (trumpets and guitars) come over to play for him. We were surprised when he had them play: America, God Bless America and America the Beautiful. Two of the musicians slept near me and they said they were surprised at his request. This was the commander who allowed me to have the funeral service. He came to Japan to visit his grandparents and was drafted into their Army.

AUGUST 23 — More mail was brought into camp and it was delivered to us shortly after breakfast. This makes a total of seven letters I have received, but not much news. Our new Camp Commander arrived and gave us his introduction speech at 9:00 A.M. I read and drew in the afternoon. Later we were able to enjoy a hot bath. I visited with Thatcher, who is from the San Francisco area. He was burned out of Tokyo before coming to Niigata. We talked about the Bible and how we wanted the Lord to use us for His glory. He hopes to serve the Lord in his home church.

We have fresh meat in camp because a cow was brought into the kitchen. About 100 yards outside the camp fence on the hill north of camp they have erected a big POW sign.

AUGUST 24 — Marutzu played a softball team of Rinko and the camp officers. Marutzu won by the lopsided score of 21 to 7. I tried to play second base, but the position seemed strange.

I left the bay in the afternoon because Wendell, Feldman and several others were playing cards.

Cecil and I talked until lights out in the evening. I am considering the possibility of going to school at Waco. I'll have two years of engineering credits to transfer. We will have to see what the Lord has planned.

AUGUST 25 — Today is a red letter day. There were three flights of twelve American planes each which flew over camp, and I believe every man in camp had tears in his eyes or at least he was on the verge of tears.

The first and last flights had an H on the wings. The middle flight had a B on their wings and dropped messages calling themselves FV47. The ones with H came back with everything in ship stores on their second flight. In fact, one of the pilots brought back his barracks bag with the love letters from his wife. It certainly did make some interesting reading. The planes with the B dropped three packages. One note said that we were sure lucky because Niigata was next up for the atomic bomb, whatever that means.

Wendell and I ate a dinner with some Type K rations, and some hardtack. We were all given a ration of eight cigarettes per person, but I did not pick up my ration. We heard the planes had come off of two aircraft carriers: San Jacinto and the Lexington II.

AUGUST 26 — I held church services in the bath house this morning. There was a fairly good attendance for the services and I had the opportunity of talking to several about the importance of living for the Lord after returning to the United States. Several really want to serve the Lord and I was especially glad for Red's decision which he can do by the grace of God. He gave me his address so I can write him and maybe visit him.

The extra food from the carriers was hardtack. This had been a lazy day but one which I think was profitable.

AUGUST 27 — The planes from the two previous carriers returned to drop some more food to us. There was a group with P's on their tails, and were supposed to have come off of a carrier Bellowwood (?). We have received K rations the last three nights.

The men burned out of Tokyo said that they had heard some ships carrying American prisoners were sunk by American subs on their way to Japan. We wonder how many were our friends, or how many made it through the prison camps. It will be interesting to pick up the pieces and see the changes in the United States because of the war years.

AUGUST 28 — The one and only activity until the middle of the afternoon was a swimming party in the mid-morning.

We heard the roar of motors about 3:00 P.M. Four B-29's came over the city of Niigata and finally headed for our camp. They came over single file and dropped barrels of supplies. Two more B-29's flew over about 5:00 P.M. One dropped food here and the other plane flew toward town and probably dropped supplies at Sietetzu where the other POWs are located. The planes had a big Z on them.

Two 55 gallon barrels were welded together and filled with food. A great deal of the food stuff was ruined by the fall, but we were allowed to eat whatever broke open. A lot of cans broke open but a knife helped us open one can of peaches. Supper consisted of peaches and cocoa with an issue of two packages of cigarettes, six packages of gum and a candy bar. Several of the fellows came up and traded their candy bar to me for my cigarettes. This American food tastes beyond our fondest memories. It seems like I'm waking up out of an awful nightmare or else having a wonderful dream. The Lord has been good to watch over and protect me these past three and a half years.

AUGUST 29 — There were two B-29's with a diamond A on them which dropped food. The gathering of food off the hill has become our favorite hobby. We have to be careful to get out of the way when the planes come over. They are aiming for the target on the hillside but some of the barrels come down short of the target. We are eating six meals a day and I am putting on weight. My weight a month ago was 65 kilo (143 pounds), which was my most as a POW.

I have heard some of the men left camp to go outside.

AUGUST 30 — Rex, one of the musicians who played for the commander, has a birthday. We have had more planes today than any previous day. The planes acted very strange for a while because they did a great deal of circling around the area. They flew over the city of Niigata and flew west over the island of Sado. They were searching south of Niigata and then headed straight for camp to drop their loads of food. The planes carried insignias of "O" and "M"s.

AUGUST 31 — I laid around camp and read this morning. I volunteered to help Captain Parker clean the commissary in the afternoon. I did it so I would have something to do, as time passes very slowly. I learned that Lieutenant Boone and Wheeler are both from Colorado, so maybe our paths will cross again.

Several groups of POWs went into the city of Niigata last night, and others played cards. It seemed strange to see some of the prisoners return to camp with the Japanese guards. The ones who went through the main gate were thrown into the brig for a couple hours, but the ones who came in the west gate were allowed to remain free.

SEPTEMBER 1 — Several of us left camp this morning to go to Seitetsu camp because we wanted to see Cisco (Cecil's uncle), Simpson, and some of the other friends in the group. We had a good visit with them before we returned to camp. We remembered to come through the side gate and not the main entrance. We have a relaxed relationship with the guards, because they are uncertain of what will happen to them. Some of them even acted friendly and we are permitted to use the west gate.

I loafed most of the afternoon and had several good visits. Most of us are making plans concerning our return to the

States. I rejoice for the attitude of the believers who desire to serve the Lord in civilian life. I tried to read the Scriptures but my eyes tire in a short time. Major Fellows left camp for a trip to Tokyo.

SEPTEMBER 2 — Bates and I decided to go down to Marutzu and the coolies recognized us. Our foremen and guards at Marutzu were not on the docks. We have noticed that almost all of those in authority over us have dropped out of sight. The camp guards have been completely changed. We decided that while we were out of camp to go over to Rinko (coal yards) and see where the other POWs had worked.

We decided to do some investigations in the afternoon. We had never been east of camp so we followed the road and then went around the hill to the left. We saw an airplane parked back in the trees off the edge of the road and climbed into the Zero. Bates was an airplane mechanic and he explained how the instruments were used and their purpose. I was glad for the lesson about the cockpit of a Zero. It was better to be on the inside of the plane, instead of looking down its gun barrel like we did on Bataan.

We went into a Japanese house-store where the front part had a little store with a few items for sale. We purchased some potatoes with some of our yen. They invited us into the home part of the building. It was poorly constructed with very little furniture. An open charcoal burner in the center of the room was for heat, to make tea, and to cook their meals. The opening of the room was a three foot square, where the shoes were to be taken off. There was a small step up to the grass mat floors. They tried to explain how they sat on the floor and would sleep on pallets. I could imagine it was hard to keep warm in the winter time. We thanked the man and two ladies for their hospitality. We exchanged bows and left their house-store.

The B-29's with a big "L" on them returned and dropped some more food.

SEPTEMBER 3 — Cecil, Red and I went out looking for nothing in particular but everything in general. We thought it was a good day to investigate the area and see what was interesting. It was good to walk about without fear of a beating. We bought some chickens, onions, potatoes and fresh corn with our hard earned yen. (They would have given them to us but we paid.) We went east of town in the afternoon and enjoyed the countryside. We did not make any purchases but stopped several times to look at produce. The food at camp is good, especially in the evening.

The B-29s came over camp and dropped food and their insignias was a "Z". Major Fellows returned to camp with some Navy officers. The group was led by Commander Harold Stassen, the former governor of Minnesota. They wore "45s" which looked good to us. They called us together and gave us a pep talk about not doing anything foolish or irrational, because it would only be a few days until we would be released.

SEPTEMBER 4 — The Navy pilots left for their base with some pictures taken. We have stayed in camp because it has been rainy. Glad for the tours of the past couple of days. We had several drops by the B-29s with "B" and "L" on them. A Japanese woman who lived close to camp was killed by a barrel. A Japanese workman on the roof was killed when the barrel landed short and went through the building. No American has been injured but several of the buildings have large holes in them where the barrels went through them.

There has been a lot of activity by the Japanese troops as they marched in and out of camp all day. We were called into a formation to hear a Japanese officer. He told us that if we wanted to stay in Japan, the Japanese government would try to arrange it for us. Boy, did we give him the horse laugh.

We were informed that half of us will board a train for Tokyo and the other half will leave tomorrow. I plan to be on the train tonight and I have my belongings packed.

SEPTEMBER 5 — I caught the train last night out of Niigata. It was a comfortable ride and sunrise put us on the outside edge of Tokyo. It was mid-morning by the time we arrived in the city proper. I saw the unbelievable destruction of Tokyo. Almost every building has been destroyed with only a few solitary walls standing, and a few shacks built out of corrugated metal. The men who had been bombed out had tried to describe the destruction. It looked like what the explosions missed, the fires finished.

We went through Kawasaki and Shinagaua on our way to Yokohama, where we were turned over to the American forces. It was wonderful to see Old Glory and the American forces. One of the first groups we saw was the First Cavalry which had been stationed at Fort Bliss, Texas. There was a large hospital ship with a big red cross on its side in the harbor and anyone who failed the physical examination was taken to the hospital ship. There were a number of medics who were ready for us. One nurse asked if there was anything she could do to help, and one of the men told her to go stand by the side of the building so that we could look at her because she was the first American lady we had seen for a number of years.

We had practically everything taken away from us. I was able to salvage a few keepsakes. We were processed, debugged, deloused, given a medical examination, and received a brand new uniform. We were taken over to some trucks and left the dock area for the airfield.

We arrived at the airfield at 4:00 P.M. I was loaded onto a C-54B, # 272569, and we took off of the field. The pilot flew low over Mount Fuji where some people were hiking up the side of the mountain and it was a good parting sight to Japan. We arrived in Okinawa about 9:30 P.M.

I thought I was really dreaming when I got off of the plane. I thought I was looking at the Milky Way because our plane was met by General Stillwell. We saluted him, but he would not return the salute. He told us that we did not have to salute anybody and if we were questioned, we could tell them that by the order of "General Stillwell, we were not to salute." I will take him at his word. We were taken over to a kitchen for cocoa and donuts. Then, we were taken to a P.O.W. Camp to be fed with cold cuts. The end of a perfect day and a thank you to the Lord for His wonderful watchcare during the years as a Japanese prisoner of war.

SEPTEMBER 6 — I spent the day relaxing in Okinawa. I went to a chapel service in the afternoon where I met Chaplain Brooks, who once was stationed at Fort Bliss. There is a good feeling to meet others who were where we had our training. We can look up at the tombs, where the Japanese hid and had to be blasted out. I am ready to continue the journey home, a dream come true. It is a time to be thankful.

SEPTEMBER 7 — I relaxed in camp but we anxiously await a plane for our journey homeward. It was good to see some of the men out of Battery E, but they only knew about others in their Japanese camp. I walked over to the Marine cemetery today. There were sure a lot of lives lost here on Okinawa. I wonder if I knew any of them or how many. I understand the

113

tombs mentioned yesterday were actually places of worship. A typhoon has been reported headed in this direction therefore a rumor states that we will leave Okinawa tomorrow.

SEPTEMBER 8 — The word was accurate about leaving Okinawa by air. We went to the airfield and boarded a B-24 shortly after noon. One of the officers asked me if I would like to sit up with the officers. I had a seat across from the Navigator and behind the pilot. I was able to watch the charting of the course, which was very interesting to me. The rest of the liberated P.O.W.s sat down by the bomb bay door. I was warned not to push or pull certain levers, because some of the other P.O.W.s would be dropped out of the plane.

The number two engine quit and the other one on that side was sputtering. The Flight Engineer was kept busy feathering the engines. The pilot told us if we had to ditch the plane, we could jump or pancake with him. I told him that I would stay with him in the plane. We were a little over halfway to the Philippines, so were at that point of no return.

We finally arrived in the Philippines near Lingayen but the pilot had never been there. He said that he thought he could see the field, which was a steel mesh landing strip. I watched him pick the place to land and it all looked like a giant rice paddy. He landed and it was the landing field. We caught another plane to Manila which was a C-47. The flight to Manila was very low over the central Luzon plains.

SEPTEMBER 9 — We were taken out to the Replacement Center at Luguna, which is fairly close to Cavite and straight east of the island of Corregidor. Someone said it was twenty nine miles south of Manila. We spent most of the time receiving clothes and in relaxation. Cecil heard his brother, Wallace, was stationed at this base and we located him in the late afternoon.

I went to the Chapel services today. I met a Christian nurse and later saw her in the Recreation center. She asked me what I thought of the new songs. One was playing and I said that it sounded like a nice tune. She had a smile and said, "Don't Fence Me In". I was ready to tell her that I did not need any wise-cracks, but fortunately I did not answer. I was glad I kept my mouth closed because that was actually the name of the song. I guess we have a tendency of being sensitive.

SEPTEMBER 10 — We waited around for processing and finally were given another medical examination in the afternoon. Cecil, Elbert, Wallace and I spent the evening talking and heard some of the news from home, which was Waco, Texas because all of them were from there. Wallace was able to tell about their family and gave us some general news from the United States.

SEPTEMBER 11 — We went through another processing in the morning. I had to give them some information, so our Service Records could be brought up to date. I received $162.00 in the afternoon for spending money until our records are processed. Cecil, Wallace and I went to a little barrio close to camp to shop. I weighed 176 pounds which means that I have gained more than two pounds a day on the American diet.

SEPTEMBER 12 — I went to the PX (Post Exchange) to buy a watch, billfold, and a few other items. I caught a truck taking G.I.s into Manila. I want to find out what happened to some of the missionaries I knew before the war changed the Philippines. I was told that both of the pastors at First Baptist had died in prison camp. (Later I heard that Brother Palmer had died but that Brother Roberts lived through prison and returned to North Carolina.) The Brooks family all made it through the war years and are well. The family departed for the States, but hope to return to the Philippines. I am the first P.O.W. interned in Japan to ask about the missionaries. Thus, there is no news concerning Jesse Miller or the other believers, who stayed in the Brooks home.

I met a Mr. Brush, who had attended Denver University, so I asked a few questions about Denver but we did not have any common friends. It was late by the time I returned to camp.

SEPTEMBER 13 — We are in the army system of hurry up and wait. We are still waiting for the ship to take us home. There are more liberated P.W.s arriving every day and good to see some of our friends from past days. Some more of the men out of Battery E have survived.

Medals were awarded and it was strange to receive a good conduct medal for being a prisoner of war for three and a half years. I received my orders that I am a Staff Sergeant, as they promoted us one rank. Our ratings were froze when captured. They would not record my specialty number from the control system because they would have had to give me a higher rank.

The four of us went to a barrio to eat egg foo young. I think we missed milk and eggs the most. Eggs are a dollar a piece but worth it.

We met several guerillas during the Japanese occupation. One of them had been at Cabcaben at the time of the surrender of Bataan. It was interesting to hear about their part in the war years and how they managed to escape capture.

SEPTEMBER 14 — We try to keep busy until we receive the orders for the ship home. The greatest excitement happens when shipping orders are posted, as we have no desire to miss the ship.

I have seen several of the men out of old Battery E. We had a report that Stephens escaped into the jungles, joined the guerillas for a number of months, but was captured and killed by the Japanese. I have not heard anything concerning Bill Moore.

SEPTEMBER 15 — I have made a path to the bulletin board to check the shipping list. I have tried to update my roster of Battery E of the deaths and survivors. We have not received any mail since we arrived in the Philippines. Sent a couple of letters home but will probably beat them there.

SEPTEMBER 16 — I have been in Replacement Center for a week. I attended Church and greatly enjoyed the fellowship but was surprised at the low attendance. I took it easy in the afternoon, and went with the Uzzels to the main base chapel in the evening.

SEPTEMBER 17 — I stayed close to the camp until the afternoon. It was announced that a shipping list was posted but I was not on it. I went to get Cisco, because he was on the list. I was ready for supper when another list was posted and my name was on it. I was assigned to a ship by the name of the U.S.S. Hugh Rodman and will leave tomorrow. The Uzzels and I went into Alabang to get some sewing done on our uniforms.

SEPTEMBER 18 — We are getting ready to leave for the ship. We boarded some trucks around 10:30 A.M. for the trip into Manila and went to the port area. It was around 4:00 P.M. when we boarded the U.S.S. Hugh Rodman. I was assigned to

Compartment 22, Bunk 104 which was between Bob Wheeler and Joe Pasquel. It is a large compartment and all are ex-prisoners of war.

SEPTEMBER 19 — We finally pulled anchor and sailed out of Manila at 1:00 P.M., after the ship refueled in Manila Bay. We went past Corregidor and the island looks barren after the many bombs and shells which landed on that little piece of real estate. It was good to put out to sea through the inland waters of the Philippines.

SEPTEMBER 20 — We have cleared the San Bernardino Straits and there is no land in sight. We are headed primarily east but a little toward the south. We arrived in the Philippines to spend four months but we are only six days short of four years.

SEPTEMBER 21 — Joe Pasquel was appointed the Sergeant Major of our group and he made me his clerk in charge of rosters and commissary. Joe was from Denver and was placed in Battery E until we arrived overseas. He was placed on Detached Service with USAFFE and made Master Sergeant. My duties include taking orders for the things purchased at the ship's store and then pass them out to the buyers. I take orders tonight for delivery tomorrow.

Liberated POWs are allowed to go back for seconds as many times as desired. We are taking advantage of the opportunity.

SEPTEMBER 22 — I have appreciated the opportunity of keeping the roster and taking the orders for commissary. It gives me something to do and helps pass the time while at sea. Some of the men did not want their allowable ration of candy, so I purchased theirs. I have five and a half boxes (132 by actual count) of Baby Ruths.

I attended Chapel services on the ship. I have spent a lot of time on the deck of the ship watching the flying fish stirred up by the ship.

SEPTEMBER 23 until OCTOBER 1 — I have decided to summarize the remaining days of the trip. The two weeks or more aboard a ship crossing the ocean has many similar days, each one like the previous day.

The ship has been going in a southeasterly direction. We

made a stop at some island for a few hours and a few boats came out to transfer the cargo. An old Navy man said the island was in the Carolina group located barely on the south side of the equator. The ship headed into a northeasterly direction upon leaving the island. A couple days later we crossed the International Date Line, so we regained the day we lost going the other direction. One of the men said that it was his birthday, so he was able to celebrate for two days.

Every day I try to read a portion of the New Testament, a few chapters at a time. My eyes seem to be improving, but they still get tired after about twenty minutes of reading. The commissary orders are less each day, so my duties are fewer.

We are satisfied with less food and the first time through the line is usually sufficient. If the men go back for seconds, it is usually for a certain dish. I have not heard anything about the two weeks of special menus that we all planned in Cabanatuan. The American diet has taken away the craving, but there are some special things which I plan to eat; a thick malted milk at Purity and a burnt sugar pie.

I want to put down a few of my thoughts. First, I realize many changes have taken place in the States. Wallace has given me a little understanding of the number of men our ages who have died or been seriously injured in action, and many lives have changed. When I arrive back in the States I will call home and find out about many friends. I want to know about the folks, some of my closest friends, those of the Mission and Tabernacle groups, and our relatives. When Cecil found Wallace in the Philippines, I thought it would have been interesting if I had met one of my cousins or close friends.

School will be very important. I want to study the Bible, so maybe I will check out the schools in Texas, or with Fred about Northwestern; or if I do return to Colorado University it will be to finish there and then go to a Seminary; but I will wait on the Lord for those decisions. I would like to start in January. The decisions may also depend on how long the Army keeps us before discharge.

September has gone. It looks like we have missed Hawaii and will sail directly into San Francisco. We have not seen any flying fish for several days, which means we are getting into colder water. The grapevine has a rumor that we are scheduled to dock day after tomorrow, or October 3rd.

It has been gracious of the Lord to spare my life. Truly He has a purpose to have watched over me during all the time of danger in these past four years. He has provided for me in every way and I can only thank Him and the men He brought into my pathway when I needed them. I could never have made it without the Lord nor for the friends he used to give help. Our main duties are to keep our area clean. Tomorrow will be the third and we are to come under the Golden Gate early in the morning. There will not be much sleep tonight because we have talked a great deal about the day we sail under the Golden Gate. Then we will truly realize we are in California. Tomorrow will be the third and my next writing should be after we have arrived at our destination.

CONCLUSION

HOME, SWEET HOME, AT LAST

The round trip is almost over after a journey of a little over four years. Tomorrow - manana - ashita: whatever the language those words carry a great message. We have been living for the tomorrows for the last forty-nine months and it is almost here, we are to dock in San Francisco.

Yesterdays are for memories—good and bad. The good memories were for the hopes of survivors who were able to return to the freedoms of home. The bad memories recalled the comrades left behind in the foreign soil or the small boxes of ashes of friends who died in Japan. My years of service divides itself into three sections; Fort Bliss, the two years connected with the Philippines and the last two years in Niigata, Japan.

The first was at Fort Bliss in the Induction Center for three weeks until I was shipped across the road to the 200th C.A. (A.A.), formerly the New Mexico National Guard. There was boot camp with hours of drills, the use of the rifle and machine gun, drawing firing tables and target practice where we had the highest score of the Anti-Aircraft units using 30 caliber machine guns. The prize was to take guns to the Orient to train natives and return in January. We took a trip around the state of New Mexico shortly before we were to go overseas. The long train ride ended at Angel Island, which was supposed to be as secure as Alcatraz.

The second stage started as we boarded the luxurious liner the U.S.S. President Coolidge from San Francisco for the Orient. Five days later, we enjoyed about six hours liberty in Honolulu. Suddenly we were joined by several naval warships and began a zig-zag course across the Pacific and then a string of islands until we entered Manila Bay. Men were waving to us from an island, which we later learned was Corregidor. The trip to Fort Stotsenburg (Clark Field) brought us to our assignment along the edge of Clark Field where mornings were spent digging in our equipment and afternoons resting from the tropical heat.

Then came the war. Clark Field was hit a couple of hours after Pearl Harbor. My tentmate was killed among many others the first day of the war. A month of retreats followed until we arrived on Bataan where we had three and a half months of constant bombing. I was glad that I was our platoon's scout, scouting mostly for extra food for my platoon. Short rations and disease took their toll as we prepared for the final battle and annihilation.

We were surrendered. We began the march out of Bataan into San Franando. There was the train ride to Capas and the walk out to O'Donnell where we stayed for the first seven weeks and then on to Cabanatuan. There were seventeen months of disease without medicine, starvation, unsanitary conditions, suffering, beatings, a constant battle for life and only about half the men continued among the living. I was assigned to a detail headed for Japan: where we wondered if it would be an improvement or greater abuse in the homeland of our enemy.

The third stage was in the land of Japan. Memories of the crowded conditions aboard the ship—twelve men in a space ten feet square. Dangers at sea which could lead to a watery grave and emergency surgery of a fellow P.O.W. in the hold of the ship and I was thankful for arrival in a Japanese port of Moji City. It was a three day train ride to Niigata where we labored for the Japanese.

The following two years were spent on the docks of Niigata, throwing pig-iron from morning until dark or loading or unloading almost anything: from 200 pound bags of beans, fish, freight, or produce but never completely away from pig-iron. We were expected to do heavy work on a very limited diet. We constantly attempted to smuggle food stuff into camp which sometimes succeeded but often ended in punishment. There was the continual threat of beatings. The first bombers dropped loads of mines in the harbor and the attack on the docks was welcomed. A few months later the guards talked about something important happened by a B-29. Then came the day we were allowed to stay in camp and then a sudden changing of our guards, American food was dropped by B-29s and the taste of American food was wonderful. Then we were liberated out of Niigata, to Tokyo and turned over to American troops. We flew to the Philippines and finally I boarded the U.S.S. Hugh Rodman.

Tomorrow - what is in store? What are the changes of the past four years? Only about a quarter of us who went to the Philippines would return. Sleep was not easy as our mind raced around the halls of memory and the prospects of new unknown paths. I wanted to be on top deck by the time the dawn broke across the eastern sky and I would view the sight of the Golden Gate, as it is outlined in the early morning fog of the Bay area.

We arrived in the States early the morning of October 3, 1945. There is one more memory that involved the Golden Gate Bridge. We had often talked about the day when we could look up and see the Golden Gate—then we would know without a shadow of doubt that we were safely home. The morning we arrived in San Francisco, I was on the deck of the ship by about 4:00 A.M. and I was not the first one there. We were wild with joy as the Golden Gate Bridge came into sight, even though it was partly obscured by fog. We saw it for only a short time but it looked wonderful. Most of us were crowded onto the deck ahead of time so we would not miss it, but a man I had worked with at Marutzu in Niigata rushed out on the deck - too late.

"Where is it?", he shouted. "Where is the Golden Gate?"

We had to tell him that we had already passed under it.

"Too late! Too late!" What tragic words!

This is a very trivial incident in comparison to that of the countless millions of men and women who want to go to Heaven, but keep putting off acceptance of the Lord Jesus Christ as their personal Savior. They will realize that they waited until it was too late!

I hope all who read this experience will accept Jesus Christ as their personal Savior today? *"Jesus saith unto him, I am the way, and the truth, and the life: no man cometh unto the Father, but by me." JOHN 14:6*

Only God can forgive sin, and Christ is God. Each of us need to realize that when Christ died on the cross He died for each one individually. He died for my sin. When He was buried, my sins were buried with Him. When He arose, the entire debt of my sins was paid. It is with our hearts that we believe unto righteousness. Will you make the Lord your Shepherd? Will you trust Him as your personal Savior?

It was wonderful to pull up beside the docks of San Francisco, and we knew that we were home in America. I was the seventh person off of the ship. A General met us, shook our hands, and welcomed us back home. We were taken to Letterman General Hospital which is located at the southern abutment of the Golden Gate Bridge.

I was assigned to a ward and given a general medical check

122

up. I would stay a few days and then be sent to a hospital in my home state, which was Fitzsimmons in Denver and only three miles from my home. I spent a few more days while the government finished processing papers and gave me more medical examinations. I tried to catch up on events in the States by reading newspapers and asking for information about America.

The first night we were allowed to go to the Communication Center and telephone home. It was good to hear my mother's voice and she was happy to hear from her wandering son. A lot of things had changed, and she said she would go into more detail when I arrived back in Denver. Dad had passed away in 1943 from a poisonous gas in a defense plant. My childhood friend, Rush, had been in the Air Force in England and had made it through the war in good shape. All of my first cousins survived the war and some of them had been in dangerous areas of combat.

The first night of sleeping in a soft comfortable bed was an experience. I was unable to rest because it was impossible to sleep in such luxury after four years of sleeping on the ground or floor. The only men who were able to sleep took a blanket and slept on the floor. Maybe in time, we would adjust to the comforts of home.

Joe's brother contacted him and we made arrangements for the three of us to drive to Denver in the Pasquel's car. We were told that Letterman would release us in about a week so the brother made arrangements to start his furlough when we could travel.

I went into San Francisco several times. I enjoyed watching a baseball game, where a one armed man by the name of Gray was playing. He played in the major leagues during the war years. He would catch the ball, toss it in the air and take off the glove from under his arm pit, catch the ball and throw it into the infield. I looked for a Baptist church in San Francisco on Sunday but could not find one so I attended a Presbyterian church.

The day arrived for the Pasquels and me to head for Denver. We drove constantly until the lights of Denver were seen and soon we stopped in front of my home.

Home sweet home, a reality and not a dream. Someday I will have another home coming in glory and it will also be a reality.

GLOSSARY

AMOEBIC — The worst and usually the final stage of several tropical diseases. Malaria and dysentery were the worst and a person lost all body control.

ANOPHELES — The female anopheles mosquito carries the malaria germ.

BAKA — The Japanese word for stupid, idiot, ignorant. A similar word in Japanese to call a person a fool is BAKAYARO.

BARRIO — A village in the Philippines.

BATAAN — A peninsula on the west coast of Manila Bay.

BENJO — Japanese word for bathroom.

BYOKI — Sick or ill with disease.

CABANATUAN — The main POW camp in the Philippines. It is about 100 miles north of Manila.

CABCABEN — The front lines on the eastern front of Bataan at the surrender and the nearest point to Corregidor.

CALESA — A popular type of vehicle in the Philippines, so are jitneys.

CELLUTITIS — A type of disease of the cells.

COBON REED — An elephant type grass which grows very high and thick.

FLAGELLANT — A mutilation of the body with the idea that sins can be forgiven by the ceremony.

HAN — Rice.

HARA-KIRI — A Japanese way of committing suicide. A knife is used to open up the midsection of the body and the knife is drawn across then upward.

HAITAI — Soldier.

HONEYCART — The nickname given to carts carrying human waste matter and taken out to be used on crops.

HORIO — Prisoner.

ICHTHYOUL — A tar product used on infections.

IGUANA — A type of lizard and it tastes similar to chicken.

KAMIKAZES — A Japanese suicide pilot.

KOMOTE — They are about a second grade sweet potato in the Philippines.

LATRINE — A military bathroom.

LUZON — The main northern island of the Philippines and the island where Manila is located.

LUGAO — Rice mush and very soupy.

MARUTZU — The shipping company of Japan and my group worked on their docks.

MITSUBISHI — The company which made the Japanese bombers.

MUGI — Barley.

NIIGATA — The city where I lived for two years in Japan and the next city up for the atomic bomb.

NIPA — The type of material used for buildings in the Philippines.

OHAYO — Good morning.

P.X. — The general store on an army base.

QUAN — A term used by POWs to describe any extra cooking and sometimes to speak about any extra food.

RINKO — The company in charge of coal yards in Niigata.

SEN — The small coin used in Japan. 100 sen = 1 yen = 50 cents American during the war years.

SENSO — War.

SHOSHO — Little, small.

SIETETZU — The steel mills and taken from the word for pig-iron or steel.

SWALLIE — Woven pieces of bamboo to make a mat. It is used for a building material to be used on the sides and sometimes for the floors.

TAKUSAN — Many or plenty.

TENKO — The Japanese word for roll call.

YEA-HOE BASKETS — Two baskets are hung on a pole. They are filled with about anything and then it takes practice to carry the full baskets.

YASUMI — Rest or a holiday.

YASUMU — Rest in sleep.

ZEROS — The main airplane of the Japanese.

ISBN 155395078-X

9 781553 950783